WISCONSIN HISTORY TIMELINE

1634	Jean Nicolet: First known European to reach Wisconsin, seeks Northwest Passage.
1661	Father Rene Menard: First missionary to Wisconsin Indians.
1673	Louis Joliet and Father Jacques Marquette discover Upper Mississippi River.
1764	Charles Langlade settles at Green Bay, area's first permanent settlement. Fur trade expands.
1783	Following Treaty of Paris, United States takes control of Wisconsin region from Britain.
1818	Solomon Juneau buys trading post at Milwaukee. Steamboats on Mississippi River.
1822	New York Indians (Oneida, Stockbridge, Munsee, and Brothertown) move to Wisconsin.
1832	Black Hawk War (future presidents serve in Wisconsin area, including Abraham Lincoln).
1833	Treaty with Indians clears south Wisconsin lead lands. First newspaper, *Green Bay Intelligencer,* published.
1836	Wisconsin Territory is formed. Belmont is capital. First permanent capital, Madison, is established the next year.
1848	Wisconsin becomes 30th state. Gov. Dewey is inaugurated. UW incorporates. Germans immigrate.
1849	School code is adopted. First free, tax-supported, graded school with high school opens at Kenosha.
1850	State opens Wisconsin Institute for Education of the Blind at Janesville.
1851	First railroad train—Milwaukee to Waukesha. First state fair, at Janesville.
1852	School for Deaf opens at Delavan. Prison construction begins at Waupun.
1853	State death penalty abolished.
1854	Republican Party is named at Ripon meeting. Joshua Glover, fugitive slave, is arrested at Racine.
1861-65	91,379 Wisconsinites serve in Union Army during Civil War; killed: 12,216.
1864	State's first cheese factory is opened, in Fond du Lac County, by Chester Hazen.
1868	C. Latham Sholes, Kenosha, invents typewriter.
1871	Peshtigo Fire burns much of six counties in northeast Wisconsin; more than 1,000 deaths.
1872	Wisconsin Dairymen's Association begins at Watertown.
1898	5,469 Wisconsinites serve in Spanish-American War; killed: 134.
1901	First Wisconsin-born governor, Robert La Follette Sr., takes office. Legislative Reference Library opens, a model for the Library of Congress.
1913	Direct election of Wisconsin's U.S. senators is approved.
1917	Capitol (burned in 1904) is completed. 122,215 Wisconsinites serve in WWI; killed: 3,932.
1919	18th Amendment (Prohibition) is ratified and then repealed in 1933.
1920	19th Amendment (Women's Suffrage) is ratified.
1923	Wisconsin State Association of Colored Women's Club begins.
1932	Wisconsin is first state to pass unemployment compensation act.
1941-45	332,200 Wisconsinites serve in WWII; killed: 8,390.
1950-53	132,000 Wisconsinites serve in Korean Conflict; killed: 729.
1958	UW's Joshua Lederberg wins Nobel Prize in medicine (UW's Howard Temin shares 1975 Nobel in medicine.)
1960	Mrs. Dena Smith is elected state treasurer, first woman elected to statewide office in Wisconsin.
1963	Wisconsin's John Gronouski is appointed U.S. Postmaster General.
1968	Wisconsin's first heart transplant and first successful bone marrow transplant performed at UW.
1969	UW Black Studies/antiwar protests. State's Melvin Laird is named Secretary of Defense. Interstate highway built.
1970	Army Mathematics Research Center at UW-Madison is bombed by antiwar protesters; one death.
1971	Merger of UW and State University systems. Revision of municipal employee relations laws.
1974	Democrats gain control of both houses of the 1975 legislature for the first time since 1893.
1964-75	165,400 Wisconsinites serve in Vietnam War; killed: 1,239.
1976	Court orders integration of Milwaukee schools. Shirley Abrahamson is first female on state Supreme Court.
1977	Gov. Patrick J. Lucey is appointed Ambassador to Mexico. No-fault divorce law is passed.
1978	Cameras are allowed in courtrooms. Vel Phillips is elected secretary of state, first black constitutional officer.
1979	School of Veterinary Medicine established at UW-Madison. Governor Lee Dreyfus employs economic indexing.
1980	Madison's Eric Heiden wins 5 Olympic Gold Medals, Sullivan Award. 15,000 Cubans are housed at Ft. McCoy. Patrick Lucey is Independent vice presidential candidate.
1984	Indian hunting/fishing rights are contested. First state liver transplants are performed at UW. "Right-to-die" law is enacted.
1986	Farmland values drop. Laws set sulfur dioxide emission limits, raise drinking age to 21.
1987	Pari-mutuel betting/lottery in. Seatbelt law enacted. G. Heileman Brewing Co. taken over by Alan Bond.
1990	More than 10,400 Wisconsinites serve in Gulf War; killed: 11.
1993	Wisconsin's Les Aspin and Donna Shalala named to U.S. Cabinet. California surpasses Wisconsin as #1 milk producer, but Wisconsin is still #1 cheese producer.
1997	Groundbreaking for Miller Park, future new home of Milwaukee Brewers baseball team.
1998	Tammy Baldwin first state Congresswoman. U.S. Supreme Court upholds Milwaukee school voucher extension. Truth-in-sentencing, fetus protection passed.
1999	Supermax prison opens at Boscobel.
2000	Legislature approves local sales tax/revenue bonds for renovation of Packers' Lambeau Field.
2001	Gov. Tommy Thompson named U.S. Secretary of Health and Human Services. Limited embryonic stem cell research allowed, UW-Madison.
2002	James Doyle elected governor, works on budget, with expansion of Indian gaming compacts.

EDITOR'S PREFACE AND ACKNOWLEDGMENTS

Developing Ideas

David J. Marcou

The group I direct, which grew out of the writing classes I still occasionally teach and the photography classes I hope to teach again, has published ten books since 1993, including this year's *Spirit of Wisconsin*. The American Writers and Photographers Alliance (AWPA), our group's new name, is proud of all our books, but this one in particular, because it is close to home yet reaches out to others widely. In other words, we are building bridges of destiny with this book; that has been our idea ever since this group self-published its first little cookbook-style literary anthology, dedicated to Shelley Goldbloom, the first teacher of the writing classes I've taught since 1993. This time, we are especially tapping into the Wisconsin Idea, which has been in the air here for more than a century—the idea that the University of Wisconsin's borders are the cultural equivalent of the geographic borders of this state, and its realm of service, as a laboratory of democracy, affects the entire world. Our group includes several professors who have strong ties to our state's universities and colleges, with impacts beyond.

Spirit of La Crosse, a grassroots history of our headquarters city, and *Spirit of America,* a literary-photographic anthology that won the September 12th Initiative's top book award in 2002, were also thorough, beautiful books, though they didn't make the *New York Times* Bestsellers List. We're still working on achieving that list, because we believe in great strength emerging from underdogs. In fact, this book, which we hope readers will think is beautiful in conception, creation, editing, design, printing, binding, distribution, and marketing, is, like our previous books, a product of communal artistry and real-world economics; we love good black-and-white reproductions and think that what you see and read here will meet with your approval.

We hope readers will understand why we think the spirit of the land and people of Wisconsin are worthy of success and acclaim. Incidentally, we've made a great effort to include this state's living governors in this book, because they have led/lead Wisconsin well. It's always been our implicit goal to be nonpartisan, or at least bi-partisan, in our books, and we believe we've done that again here.

We thank all of the contributors, both regionally and internationally known, including all eight living governors of Wisconsin, and our families and friends, the production staff (especially our book's designer, printer, and publisher), our booksellers, our reviewers, and all of you buyers and readers of our new book—a volume we hope will have many people saying after they've read it, "That really *is* the Spirit of Wisconsin." We will all be happy about it then—and hopeful not only for Wisconsin's future, but for America's and the world's.

Enjoy our new book ... we have enjoyed producing it for you!

SPIRIT OF WISCONSIN

A Historical Photo-Essay of the Badger State

Edited by David J. Marcou
for the American Writers and Photographers Alliance,
with Prologue by Former Governor Lee S. Dreyfus,
Introduction by Former Governor Patrick J. Lucey,
Foreword by Governor James Doyle,
and Technical Advice by Steve Kiedrowski

CONTENTS

Wisconsin History Timeline 3

Preface and Acknowledgments 4
David J. Marcou

1 Birth of the Republican Party 5
Former Governor Lee S. Dreyfus

2 Rebirth of the Democratic Party . . . 6
Former Governor Patrick J. Lucey

On Wisconsin! 7
Governor James Doyle

Wisconsin in the World 8
David J. Marcou

We Are Wisconsin 18
Professor John Sharpless

3 Wisconsin's Natural Heritage 26
Jim Solberg

4 Portraits and Wisconsin 36
Dale Barclay

5 Athletes, Artists, and Workers 44
Steve Kiedrowski & David J. Marcou

6 Faith in Wisconsin 54
Fr. Bernard McGarty

7 Wisconsinites Who Serve 62
Daniel J. Marcou

8 Communities and Families 72
tamara Horstman-Riphahn & Ronald Roshon, Ph.D.

9 Wisconsin in La Crosse 80
Anita T. Doering

10 Wisconsin in America 90
Roberta Stevens

11 America's Dairyland 98
Patrick Slattery

12 Health, Education & Philanthropy . . . 108
Kelly Weber

13 Firsts and Bests 116
Nelda Liebig

14 Fests, Fairs, and Fun 126
Terry Rochester

15 Seasons and Metaphors of Life 134
Karen K. List

Building Bridges of Destiny 144
Yvonne Klinkenberg

Spirit of Wisconsin: A Historical Photo-Essay of the Badger State

Copyright © 2005—for entire book: David J. Marcou and Matthew A. Marcou;
for individual creations included in/on this book: individual creators.

ISBN: 0-9674740-7-8

> "I can have talent and vision, but without the subject I have nothing."
> – *NATIONAL GEOGRAPHIC* PHOTOGRAPHER ROBB KENDRICK

> "State history is a difficult medium."
> —ROBERT C. NESBIT, *Wisconsin: A History*

> "Yesterday is gone. Tomorrow has not yet come. We have only today. Let us begin."
> —BLESSED MOTHER TERESA

STAFF

Publisher: Speranza LLC, Kalamazoo, Michigan, Co-Owners: Sean and Rebecca Niestrath.

Project Director and Editor: David J. Marcou, Director, American Writers and Photographers Alliance.

Technical Advisor: Steve Kiedrowski.

Business Advisors: David A. and Rose Marcou.

Photo-Scanners/Computer Experts: Bob Mulock, Bob's Moen Photo; Matthew A. Marcou.

ner and Copy Editor: Sue Knopf, Graffolio.

Printer: Walsworth Publishing Company, Marceline, Missouri.

Commentators: Mary Ann Grossmann, David McCullough, John Whale, Sean Louth, Richard Boudreau.

Creative Contributors: Credited within.

Financial Sponsors: Don and LaVonne Zietlow; Gary and Karmin Van Domelen; Dr. Mark and Roberta Stevens; Peter and tamara Horstman-Riphahn; Fr. Bernard McGarty; Dan and Vicki Marcou; Mike and Mary Temp; the Kiedrowski/Brom Family of Centerville; Sam McKay; Paul and Debbie Abraham; Terry and Peg Jerome; Mark and Jean Marie Smith; Carl and Nelda Liebig; Jay and Judith Hoeschler; Fr. Roger Scheckel; Tom and Joy Marcou; Laurie Reed; Dr. Robert and Carole Edland; Werner and Jolene Engel; Jim and Rita Grenisen; the La Crosse Loggers Baseball Team; WKBT-TV8; Charles and Christine Freiberg; Paul and Lilly Kosir; Brant and Louise Moore; John and Jean Wiatt; Terry and Cheryl Smith; the Recovery Room (Bruce Simones, Owner); John and Beth Satory and Satori Arts; Gary and Stephanie Coorough; John and Dee Medinger; Zita and Ed Pretasky; Mr. & Mrs. James Rubatt; Mr. & Mrs. Joe Haworth; Rocky and Diane Skifton; Lynn Sattler; Dale Barclay; Bob and Lorraine Mulock; Mariel Carlisle; Chuck and Kay Dockendorff; David W. Johns; and Judge Dennis Marcou.

For All of Our Parents
And for the Memory of Devyn Marie Doughty,
Elizabeth Martha Hampel, James Holey,
and the other great Wisconsinites, photographers,
writers, and bridgebuilders
who have gone before us.

COVER CAPTIONS

FRONT

Bridge: Two young men going west on new bridge's dedication day, Mississippi River at La Crosse, November 17, 2004, photo by David J. Marcou.

Flag: "On Wisconsin," UW-UM football game, 2002, photo by David J. Marcou.

NFL: Green Bay quarterback Brett Favre gets set to pass behind Frank Winters vs. Detroit, 1990s, photo and copyright by Vernon J. Biever.

Diorama: Indian hunting diorama, Milwaukee Public Museum, 1987, photo by Debbie Abraham.

BACK

"Test Pilot": Gable, Loy, and Milwaukee native (Spencer) Tracy on set of *Test Pilot*, circa 1938, MGM for Wisconsin Historical Society (ID#11012).

Experiment: Round barn in Alga Shivers' barn-building territory, Vernon County, 2004, photo by Professor Roger Grant.

Entrepreneurial genius: A Kwik Trip store, the nation's top convenience store chain in 2004, La Crosse, 2004, photo by Steve Kiedrowski.

The Wrights: Mrs. and Mr. Frank Lloyd Wright reading at Taliesin East, 1936, photo by Melvin E. Diemer for Wisconsin Historical Society (ID#3976).

TITLE PAGE

Bridge building, La Crosse, photos by John Zoerb, 2003–04.

Below: David A. and Rose Marcou repeat their wedding vows for their Golden Valentine Anniversary, with Fr. Roger Scheckel presiding and WXOW-TV19 reporting, St. James Church, La Crosse, February 2000, photo by David J. Marcou, their oldest son.

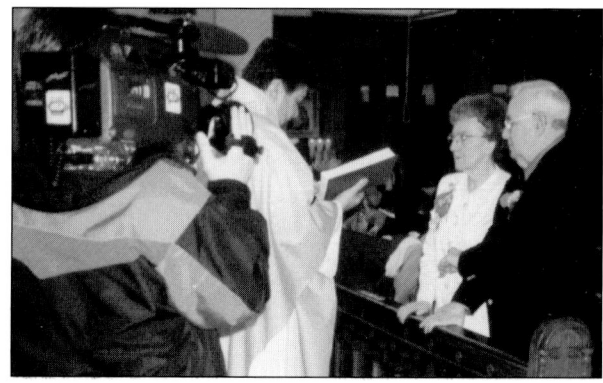

PROLOGUE

Birth of the Republican Party

Lee S. Dreyfus, Wisconsin's 41st Governor, 1979–1983

It was a blustery night in March 1854 as more than fifty men gathered in the wooden schoolhouse in Ripon. Diverse they were—Whigs, disaffected Democrats, and religious abolitionists opposed to slavery, as well as "free soilers," who opposed adding slave states as new ones formed. The addition of Maine as a free state had been balanced by the addition of Missouri as a slave state. The Democratic Party controlled Congress, and favored slavery. The Whigs were decaying. Many in the North held meetings to oppose Southern Democrats. Alan Bovay of Illinois organized Ripon's meeting, and Ripon became the birthplace of the Republican Party, for at that meeting the party got its name.

Just six years later, the new party had spread across the North and would win the presidency with candidate Abraham Lincoln of Illinois. The Republican Party would capture the presidency for all but twelve of the next fifty-two years. In 1855, Coles Bashford of Fond du Lac became our first Republican governor. Between then and today, all but ten of our thirty-nine succeeding governors have been Republicans. As we look at third parties today, no new party since can say that within six years of its founding, it controlled the presidency, the Congress, and the executive branches of half of the nation, as the Republican Party did in the mid-nineteenth century.

Today there are disagreements between moderate and conservative Republicans, with the conservatives clearly in control in early 2005, but the Republican Party has always been a two-wing party. Despite early successes, the party was seriously divided from the start—into Unionists and Abolitionists—and threatened Lincoln's re-election. Lincoln understood that the Union needed to be preserved before slavery could be abolished; both would be accomplished. By the 1880s, the two wings had morphed into the Stalwarts, representing industry, and Robert La Follette's Progressives, representing farmers and the working class. That squabble went on through my administration in the early 1980s, to Governor Tommy Thompson's tenure, 1987-2001, when he was able to make his policies and performance acceptable to both wings through his exceptional political skills. After fourteen years in office, Governor Thompson was called to Washington to be in the Cabinet, and the party's split resurfaced—now as Moderates and Neocons (for New Conservatives).

This long tradition of two wings in one party is the basis for its continuing vigor and strength. A century and a half ago at its birth in Ripon, a debut of great national significance, the Republican Party had vigor from the clash of Abolitionists and Unionists. Later, it was the clash of Stalwarts and Progressives. Today it is the clash of Moderates and Neoconservatives. Tomorrow it may be some other split, because the spirit of Wisconsin prefers conflict over conformity and clash over unity. It's good for America that the Republican Party began here in Wisconsin, a state known also for its independent spirit. Readers should enjoy the independent-minded *Spirit of Wisconsin*.

INTRODUCTION

Rebirth of the Democratic Party

Patrick J. Lucey, Wisconsin's 39th Governor, 1971–77

In 1946 Senator Robert La Follette Jr., a Progressive Party member, lost a primary to Joe McCarthy. Born in La Crosse, I'd just come home from the war to Ferryville, a village on the Mississippi, to work for my father. The paper I read was the *La Crosse Tribune*—mainly John Weingard's column. Many vets wanted to revitalize the Democratic Party after the Progressives' demise; but it wasn't until a Madison meeting in 1948 that I truly felt at home. I met Henry Reuss, Carl Thompson, Jim Doyle Sr., Horace Willkie, and Gaylord Nelson there.

I ran for the Assembly against Speaker Don McDowell. Prairie du Chien official Margarite Rogers told me, "Now that you are a candidate the most important thing you can do for the party is to get elected." I did, in 1949. That year in the Assembly, Democrats were outnumbered by Republicans 74 to 26—only a bit better than our twelve seats in 1947; but having Tom Fairchild as Attorney General helped. Tom was the only statewide Democrat elected since the 1930s. In 1950 he ran for Senate, I for Congress. Neither one of us won then.

Now I could have gone home and worked for Dad, or devoted myself to politics. Jim Doyle Sr. was state party chairman. He suggested I work for the party full-time, warning of the horrors if McCarthy were re-elected in 1952. I hit the road as party organizer and worked off shoe leather, staying at members' homes to trim costs. I soon was Tom's campaign manager. Once I needed to reach him. At two minutes till noon, I called a state hotel and asked if I could speak to him. The lady didn't know his name. I asked her to stay on the phone and in one minute a car would turn in front of her hotel, with a sign, "Fairchild for U.S. Senator." She shot back, "Oh yes, he's just coming around the corner now." Despite his noted punctuality, Tom lost.

McCarthy died in 1957, after Senate censure. I was state Democratic Party Chairman during the special election. I phoned Ellen, Bill Proxmire's wife, the day before, saying we wouldn't win. Ellen shouted, "But Pat, you don't understand, we are going to win!" That win was crucial. In 1958, Bill was re-elected to a full term; our ticket did well, including Gaylord Nelson and John Reynolds. John Kennedy's win in 1960 and my governorship in the 1970s didn't hurt either. After its 1950s rebirth, the Wisconsin Democratic Party today has power and influence equal to the Republican. We need two good parties. Ours is a great state, and its history and images are represented well in this book.

Spirit of Wisconsin, by the American Writers and Photographers Alliance, based in La Crosse, deserves your best attention.

FOREWORD

On Wisconsin!

Governor James Doyle

More than 150 years ago, my great-great-grandfather left Ireland for America, eventually settling on a farm in Waupun, Wisconsin, to raise his family. Thousands of others did the very same thing: They left what they knew and accepted almost unimaginable personal hardships for the promise of something better.

Some came from Ireland, others from Germany and Scandinavia. Some were fleeing slavery in the South, and others were escaping political persecution. They joined those who were already here in Wisconsin, and together, they built the Wisconsin we know and love.

And just like the Wisconsinites of today, all they ever asked for was a chance—a chance to work hard, a chance to learn, a chance to succeed.

One of the great privileges of being governor is the opportunity to tour the state and meet people from all walks of life. Almost every day, I hear stories that demonstrate the spirit of Wisconsin. Teachers who come up with innovative ways of inspiring students. Police officers and firefighters who risk their lives to protect the lives of their neighbors. And entrepreneurs who act on their dreams and launch businesses that provide jobs and create products and services that support our economy.

In churches and community centers and crowded gymnasiums across the state, I've also met families of those serving in Wisconsin's armed forces—children saying good-bye to their father, parents burying a son or a daughter. I have seen communities bear these absences with dignity and courage. And on occasions such as these, I am reminded that Wisconsin really is a family.

I am proud of Wisconsin. And to every small businessperson who took a chance on an idea, to every worker who didn't give up, to all the students who pushed a little harder, to each farmer who got up a little earlier, I am proud of what we have accomplished together. Wisconsin is on the move —providing people with a chance to work hard, a chance to learn, and a chance to succeed.

Challenges still remain, but I have faith in Wisconsin—in its people and their tremendous spirit—to meet the challenges. As you can see in the pages of this book, the greatness of our state is a testament to the hard work, determination, and character of Wisconsin's people. Let's continue working together to keep our great state moving forward.

On Wisconsin!

Bucky Badger, photo by Gary Coorough.

Wisconsin in the World

David J. Marcou

Before Columbus, vague oral accounts existed of contacts between Native Americans and the rest of the world. Mainly these occurred in legends, but no thorough written records exist of contacts between the two cultures then. Columbus sailed the ocean blue in 1492, and everything became "new."

In 1634, when Jean Nicolet set foot on the territory that would become the state of Wisconsin, he was seeking a Northwest Passage to the Pacific and Asia for France. (Lewis and Clark, though not traveling through the Wisconsin area, sought the same thing in the early nineteenth century for America.) New France was growing, and the French kings nourished their colony more by sending missionaries to convert natives than by sending settlers, given the apathy among many of the French populace for everything

Anchor and lighthouse along Lake Michigan shore, Algoma, photo by Mark Smith.

Wisconsin in the World 9

Top: La Crosse Mayor John Medinger and Governor Tommy Thompson (in suits and ties) and others gather for "Oktoberfest at the Capitol," circa 2000, courtesy of the John and Dee Medinger Family.

Left: A World Peace Flag for sister cities, courtesy of the John and Dee Medinger Family.

Wausau School District speech-language pathologist Christine Freiberg with Hmong protégés (L-R) Jerry, Andy, and TouNhia, 2003, courtesy of Charles and Christine Freiberg.

but furs and European prestige. Wars were fought often on the Continent, and men were needed back home to fight or work.

But the French weren't the only people interested in the Americas; the British, Spanish, Portugese, and Dutch were, too, not to mention the Native Americans. By the time Britain took over France's share of what would someday become the United States—and Wisconsin, in 1763—life was changing. And by 1783, when the United States won its own territory, and 1815, when it took over the Wisconsin area finally, change was accelerating. Still, it would be a hundred years before the United States and Wisconsin would be viewed as real forces for positive change in the world. In that regard, the Civil War helped a bit, but it was during World War I, when America came to the rescue of Britain and France, that the world really noticed the "United States."

Of course, Wisconsin was important before 1918 to Wisconsinites and many other Americans; it had been a gateway to the Northwestern territories and states. And its beautiful land and waterways

Left: Homage in Wisconsin to Edward Steichen's "Brooklyn Bridge," original photo in color on textured paper by John J. Satory Jr.

Below: Three Perpiches from Wisconsin visiting Guatemala, 2004, courtesy of the Dr. Mark and Sandra Perpich Family.

Elephants at the Milwaukee Zoo, photo by Debbie Abraham.

presented economic and social opportunities that immigrants, Yankees, and Native Americans capitalized on. Potential agricultural, industrial, marine, and transport profits lured all sorts of people. Today's Old World Wisconsin village and farmlands prove the value of our ancestors' lives, as it does ours now.

The facts that the Republican Party was introduced here and Progressivism was founded here brought in even more people as time went by, yet Wisconsin is not overpopulated today, partly because there still is a lot of land in farms and parks/preserves. Also, while urban centers are growing and international interest expands in America's Dairyland—home to so many attractive businesses, farms, churches, and schools—the Badger State and Wisconsinites retain many of their traditions, even as they travel everywhere in the world and navigate via the Internet.

Progressivism, which is more a cultural philosophy than a political ideology today, has been a great boon to America and the world due to the legislation and human talent it has called forth.

Wisconsin in the World   13

"Old-style" women with baskets, Old World Wisconsin, circa 1999, photo by Peg Jerome.

Chapel and hills in Wales, a future sister state? Photo by British AWPA member Margaret Salisbury, FRPS.

Trooper John J. Satory Jr. (R) and friend, Vietnam, early 1970s, courtesy of the John and Beth Satory Family.

One of its great early photographic proponents, Oshkosh-born Lewis Hine, prompted child labor legislation with studies of how the poorest of the poor lived and worked in the early twentieth century. Also passed then were unemployment and worker's compensation laws, predating the New Deal's very progressive legislation.

But whatever world press Wisconsin may have received then, it can't compare with coverage of it today. Like it or not, the American military polices much of the world now, and the troops that go through Fort McCoy, near Sparta, are numerous and have impact. Partly due to that and partly despite it, business, cultural, political, educational, and religious exchanges between our state and the world are multiplying exponentially. For instance, La Crosse has five international sister cities now—in Germany, France, China, Russia, and Ireland—and may add more. Equally positive is the relationship between Wisconsin and its sister "state," Nicaragua. The Olympics, other sports, the Peace Corps, other charitable organizations, the United Nations, and many other events and organizations also have great influence on how the world perceives us, as Americans and Wisconsinites, and we influence much of the world by our interests and actions here and abroad.

Moving into the world, all Wisconsinites should demonstrate to other peoples the best traits of humanity and evoke the human spirit. The world around us gives ample room for interactions and

Dr. James Baumgaertner reflects on Christ, Rio de Janeiro, circa 2003, photo by Peggy Baumgaertner.

Baseball lesson in Nicaragua, Wisconsin's sister state, circa 2003, photo by Rick Wood.

achievements, and it's hoped these supply many peoples and environments with the goodness we all need.

When readers think of Wisconsinites in the world, they should think, see, and feel the Spirit of Wisconsin and the capacity we have for renaissance and renewal.

Wisconsin photographers influence how others perceive us and how we perceive others. *Milwaukee Journal Sentinel* staff photographer Rick Wood, an Indiana native, has called Milwaukee home for more than twenty-five years, but he also enjoys traveling and taking photographs worldwide. A three-time Pulitzer nominee, Wood toured Nicaragua, Wisconsin's sister state, in 2003, and Cuba in 2004 and brought back many photos—of women, men, children, sports, cars, buses, bikes, carts, horses, cows, landfills, and cityscapes.

Wood has also photographed scenes of terror and turmoil in areas such as New York City on 9/11 and North Korea—and he's learned that no matter what their political systems are, people are still people wherever he goes.

Bicyclist and arch, Cuba, another future sister state? 2004, photo by Rick Wood.

We Are Wisconsin

Professor John Sharpless

The Middle West is a special "between" place—between the arboreal forests of the Canadian Shield and the misty valleys and rolling ridges of the upper southlands. It is the "middle border" between "The East" and the great "American West"—with no exact beginning or ending. To the east, the Middle West starts somewhere in the wooded hills of eastern Ohio and ends west in the "nowhere" of the Badlands and the flat prairies of Nebraska and Kansas, within reasonable range of the Great Rockies. If there's a unifying geography, it's the great drainage basin of the Mississippi, Ohio, and Missouri rivers and its northern "border"—the Great Lakes.

Of all of our nation's regions, the Middle West is the least well-defined. Its borders—its edges—are on the frontiers of the mind, not

Top: Black Hawk, or Ma-Ka-Tai-Me-She-Kia-Kiah, Saukie chief, circa 1830s, lithograph by J. T. Bowen for the Wisconsin Historical Society (ID# 3772).

Left: Aerial view of a western Wisconsin farm, photo by Tony David Kiedrowski.

We Are Wisconsin 19

Top left: Road through big woods, northern Wisconsin, circa 2004, photo by Bob Mulock.

Top right: T-6's over Wisconsin, Deke Slayton Airfest, circa 2004, photo by Dave Larsen.

Left: Seven/Main Bridge over main channel of Black River, near McGilvray Road, circa 1900, courtesy of Murphy Library, UW-La Crosse (ID #25866), with the aid of Mariel Carlisle.

Minnesota native Charles Lindbergh returns to his college, UW-Madison (Camp Randall Stadium), August 22, 1927, soon after his most historic flight, photo by Melvin E. Diemer for the Wisconsin Historical Society (ID# 5126).

on the road map. Its history seems less raucous and bold compared to the Rocky Mountain West's or New York City's. And our self-identity is less sharply articulated than the American South's. The Middle West was not born of war, national rebellion, cattle drives, or gold. If there is a common experience, it's more subtle.

But those of us who were born or have spent our lives here, well, we just know "the place," in a way, like the Native Americans have long known it. We know the rich aroma of our springs, the bite of our winters, the languid heat of our summers and riotous beauty of our autumns. We know our corn fields, prairies, and forests; our rivers, lakes, and marshlands. We know the smells and sounds of our cities. They are not like those big cities of the East and West Coasts. Ours are still a bit rough and raw, seemingly naïve and unsophisticated, as if they haven't quite grown up yet. As old and worn as they sometimes seem, though, they still are often young and filled with spirit.

Most of all, we know our people—their restraint; their quiet, often self-effacing humor; their charity without presumption of reciprocity; and their ingrained suspicion of pretense and pomposity. The Midwesterner. Who is he? Who is she? Perhaps as "bland" as the place? Not so striking a caricature as those of the East, the West, and the South. Harder to stereotype and lampoon perhaps, but nonetheless identifiable when we see and hear the type. Flat, nasal accent; broad-faced; sun-marked; and given to a quaint exaggeration in the stories they tell. Innocents tempered by hardship. Romantics guarded by cynicism lest their dreams fail them, and yet, hopeful at every turn—i.e., quintessentially American.

Top: Historic buildings and cars, UW-Madison, 1930s, courtesy of the Werner and Jolene Engel Family.

Bottom: Old barn, western Wisconsin, circa 2003, photo by Mark Smith.

The Zickermans and Freibergs at Madison's Camp Randall Stadium for UW-UM football game, November 2004, photo by Karen Zriny.

Former Green Bay Packers coach Vince Lombardi, for whom the Super Bowl's Lombardi Trophy is named, pro football writers' dinner, Milwaukee, February 10, 1969, photo by Robert C. Miller/Milwaukee Journal for the Wisconsin Historical Society (ID# 19898).

And, at the heart of the Middle West is Wisconsin—heart for the heartland—which not only gave birth to geniuses like Frank Lloyd Wright, "Fighting Bob" LaFollette, and Georgia O'Keeffe, but also raised up non-natives like Henry Aaron and Brett Favre to superstar status, and contributed to some of the most famous combat units in U.S. history, as well as hard-working farm families that supply food and drink and fabric to the world. To be sure, it is that multi-variegated peninsula jutting north out of the Illinois flatlands—Lake Superior to the north, Lake Michigan to the east, and the St. Croix and Mississippi rivers to the west.

Top: Frank Lloyd Wright's *Monona Terrace*, photo and copyright by Zane B. Williams.

Left: UW-La Crosse Textbook Rental Store workers, 2004, photo by Cory Miller.

Above: Horse collars and bridles, Stonefield Village, circa 2003, photo by Paul Abraham.

Right: Nighttime storefront with cheesehead motif, circa 1993, photo by Robert Joseph.

But what Wisconsin "is" is as vague as what makes the Middle West a "region." Sometimes it's so subtle that only people who live here know. "I can't tell you what it is, but I know it when I see it," residents say, when they've been gone a while and miss it. It can be nothing more than the smell in the air before a summer thunderstorm or an offhand reference to the political circus at the Capitol in Madison, or a verbal shot at Chicago's Bears. Sometimes it's outlandish, like plastic or foam cheesehead hats and intemperate beer-and-brat tailgate parties just outside Lambeau Field, Camp Randall Stadium, and Miller Park, where Vince Lombardi, Ron Dayne, and Robin Yount are still remembered as demigods. Sometimes it's nothing more than the sound of cicadas on a hot summer afternoon or the smell of an open fire on a cold winter morning that brings to mind what Wisconsin is to those of us who live here. The "Wisconsin Idea" used to be famous, and should be again, though somewhat redefined. A laboratory of democracy is what we were during the Progressive Era, and perhaps we are/will be again. Read this book and others to know about our government and culture.

We share much with our close neighbors, but there are also things that differentiate us, even from the adjacent states of Michigan, Illinois, Iowa, and Minnesota. Whatever the differences are (or were), subtle or obvious, there is a strong sense of pride about what we are and have. The people of Wisconsin have a state loyalty rivaled only by that of Texas. We wear our pride on our hats, shirts, jackets, coffee mugs, car bumpers, and bridges—from La Crosse to Madison to Milwaukee and around the state.

This book represents that pride, the vital feeling for place, the special nature of Wisconsin's people, its landscape and its history. This state's story is told in visual images, as well as words, for what we are is, often, what we see. This collection of images and narratives tries to answer the question: "What is it that sets Wisconsin apart, making the spirit and products of its land and people vital to America and the world?"

Living Governors

From top left down: Gaylord Nelson, 36th, 1959–63; Patrick J. Lucey, 39th, 1971–77; Martin Schreiber, 40th, 1977–79; Lee S. Dreyfus, 41st, 1979–83; Tony Earl, 42nd, 1983–87; Tommy Thompson, 43rd, 1987–2001; Scott McCallum, 44th, 2001–2003; James Doyle, 45th, 2003–; Governor Doyle speaks with construction workers; Governors Warren Knowles (deceased), Martin Schreiber, Lee Dreyfus, and Tony Earl join hands; Paul Frederick—UW-Madison student and potential governor, 2004, photo by Mary Temp via Mike Temp. We are grateful to the governors and their staffs and families for contributing these photos. The portrait of Tommy Thompson is by David J. Marcou.

Wisconsin's Natural Heritage

Jim Solberg

A badger's curiosity, 2004, photo by Jim Solberg.

Crystal clear lakes, lush green forests, sparkling streams—these are some of the first images that come to mind when Wisconsin is mentioned. The Badger State does indeed offer a rich natural heritage. Modern Wisconsin presents a blend of world-class natural treasures, agricultural diversity, and municipal and industrial development.

It is an ever-changing scene that has been evolving over thousands of years. Up until the last few centuries, the face of Wisconsin was shaped largely by nature and relatively mildly by the presence

Wisconsin's Natural Heritage

Landscape just north of Eau Claire, late 1980s, photo by Anna Motivans.

Swallowtail butterfly, photo by Mark Smith.

Two frisky squirrels, photo by Laurie Reed.

of Native Americans. The most profound physical features of the state were shaped more than ten thousand years ago by massive sheets of ice that periodically ground over the bedrock, leaving behind depressions that became our lakes and streams. The melting ice also left piles of debris that became hills and ridges of glacial soils, gravel, and boulders. The rugged features of southwestern Wisconsin—the Driftless Area—were missed by the glaciers, and are characterized by deeply dissected coulees tucked between sinuous ridges. Enormous glacial lakes burst their natural dams, creating massive floods that scoured the valleys of the Mississippi and Wisconsin Rivers, further deepening the coulees that fed into these big river systems.

The original residents of the state, arriving as the ice receded, gathered the new vegetation and hunted animals, some of which—mammoths and mastodons—are now extinct. As the land eventually dried out, the giant creatures and vast treeless tundras disappeared. Wisconsin has gradually become a fascinating potpourri of environments, including northern pine forests, deciduous woodlands, prairies, river systems, lakes, and marshes.

For several millennia after the last ice age, small groups of these early people adapted to the changing conditions by hunting rabbit, elk, and whitetail deer and netting a variety of fish species. They also gathered nuts, berries, roots, wild rice, and many kinds of leafy plants from surrounding woods and fields. About a thousand years ago, some of these people learned how

Right: Buck, photo by Jim Solberg.

Below: Deer hunting cabin, Rhinelander area, photo by Gary Van Domelen.

Canoeist in timeless silhouette, photo by Jim Solberg.

to grow their own crops, such as beans, squash, and corn, allowing them to settle in larger, more permanent villages.

They showed their respect for the spirits within the earth and the creatures upon it in many ways. Some carved pictures into the rocky cliffs, while others built earthen mounds in the shapes of bears, deer, falcons, and even turtles. Some told tales that passed from generation to generation. And many, to this day, show deep respect for their wildlife brothers by naming their clans after them.

The first Europeans to interact with the original residents were the French fur traders and missionaries. They mingled closely with the Indians by building trading posts, intermarrying, and sometimes living in Native American villages. Later, pioneers from the newly formed United States moved in, and they soon began to change the countryside. The new settlers eventually took over much of the land and began to clear large areas to grow crops and pasture animals. Towns and cities grew to supply a place for homes and industries. And soon, these pioneers began the herculean task of removing virtually all of Wisconsin's vast virgin forests.

Above: Ducks in snow, photo by Carole Edland.

Left: One-time Wisconsin resident John Muir, grandfather of the U.S. environmental movement, photographer unknown, for the Wisconsin Historical Society (ID#3948).

Eagle in flight, photo by Jim Solberg.

Northeastern Wisconsin sunset, photo by Gary Van Domelen.

This rapid pace of human progress has continued unabated, but a renewed respect for the land is also growing. Like the Native Americans before them, many Wisconsinites now see our wild heritage as a treasure in its own right. Some thoughtful people from the state, such as John Muir, Aldo Leopold, and Gaylord Nelson, have even achieved worldwide respect for their insightful messages of conservation, preservation,

Wisconsin's Natural Heritage   33

Left: Impressionistic tree reflection, Wyalusing State Park, photo by Paul Kosir, author, Wyalusing History.

Below: Sun, water, rocks, photo by Laurie Reed.

Reclining fawn, photo by Debbie Abraham.

and the wise use of wild lands and waterways. They have inspired the creation of national parks and the setting aside of large areas of wildlife habitat.

Today, many laws protect endangered wildlife, including plants, animals and habitats. The Wisconsin Department of Natural Resources, along with many other organizations, continues to protect and restore the state's natural heritage. Creatures like the wolf, the fisher (marten) and the peregrine falcon, all gone for a while from the state, now roam freely once again. We can only hope that this spirit of Wisconsin, which has pervaded the lives of the original peoples through the millennia and has touched modern conservationists in the last few decades, will enable future generations to cherish and enjoy the rich treasures nature has entrusted to us.

That is Wisconsin's natural heritage.

Lighthouse, Fond du Lac, photo by Carl Liebig.

Portraits and Wisconsin*

Dale Barclay

People say a picture is worth a thousand words. Pictures, whether they are renderings of scenes or portraits of people, give the viewer insight into the times depicted. The historian in a person can pick up clues about the lifestyle, personality, and other things about an individual—or even a generation—without fully realizing it at first.

In 1859, Steven H. Carpenter, then curator of the Wisconsin Historical Society, defined a good portrait: "A speaking portrait will often live in the remembrance of the people, and serve to retain the memory of early pioneers, far more than any written description of themselves, their lives and their labors." That is why pictures are regarded as our most prized possessions when they are threatened by tragic circumstances.

Antique photo of unknown Wisconsin woman, courtesy of the Werner and Jolene Engel Family.

---

* The pictures viewed in this chapter and book represent a selected sample of the wide range and colossal number of historical materials available to anyone interested in Wisconsin's heritage. Undoubtedly, there are many others that should be cited in passing, but space doesn't permit. Visit your local library for more information.

Portraits and Wisconsin 37

Reunion, Iron Brigade, Milwaukee Armory, September 1887, photo by H. H. Bennett for the Wisconsin Historical Society (ID #10695).

Group portrait, Coulee Region, Hmong New Year, courtesy of the John and Dee Medinger Family.

Rachel Horstman and kitten, Bangor, 1997, photo by tamara Horstman-Riphahn.

The first director of the Wisconsin Historical Society, James Draper, commissioned Samuel Brookes and his partner Thomas Stevenson to paint portraits of important people in Wisconsin history. Along with key portrait photographers, they recorded people and events relevant to nineteenth-century Wisconsin. Later, Milwaukee-raised Edward Steichen and others continued to record portraits on film and on canvas. Every state has famous people in its history, and Wisconsin is no exception, yet pictures of everyday people and their life and times are just as relevant to the state's history.

James Otto Lewis attended many important meetings with Wisconsin Indian tribes and painted portraits of these meetings under government contract in the 1830s. Returning to Philadelphia, he produced lithographs of them.

Portraits and Wisconsin 39

Governor, U.S. Senator, Progressive Party luminary, and presidential candidate Robert "Fighting Bob" LaFollette, Madison, circa 1915, photo by the DeLonge Studio for the Wisconsin Historical Society (ID #11015).

Steve Kiedrowski portraying President Millard Fillmore and Kestrel Jenkins, Miss Trempealeau, Grand Excursion, Trempealeau, 2004, courtesy of Steve Kiedrowski.

Chamber Chorale, St. Mary of the Angels Chapel, La Crosse, February 2004, photo by Professor Roger Grant.

Marcou family portrait, La Crosse, Memorial Day, 1997, photo by Matthew A. Marcou.

Immigrant photographer Andreas Larsen Dahl traveled by wagon to many Norwegian clients in south-central Wisconsin from 1869 to 1880 from his gallery in De Forest. He sold them stereopticon views (twenty-five cents each) of their farms, churches, pastors, and associations, and took portraits for their family albums.

Charles J. Van Schaick was a photographer who worked in the Black River Falls area in the late nineteenth and early twentieth centuries. He took formal portraits as well as snapshots of everyday scenes, including views of Winnebago people, families, funerals, workers, and women.

Wisconsin's tourism industry owes much to H. H. Bennett. His excellent photos of gorgeous rock formations around Wisconsin Dells helped draw early visitors there. His photographs suggested exotic lands no one had believed existed. Many people still tour that part of the Driftless Area. Bennett also photographed the everyday life of many types of people, often making portraits.

Oshkosh-born Lewis Hine became famous after moving to New York and photographing horrible working and immigrant conditions in the early twentieth century. He photographed

Portraits and Wisconsin 41

Julie Klein visiting the area of Wisconsin-based Scott Thompson's film Retroflex, *Two Harbors, Minnesota, 2004, photo by Steve Kiedrowski.*

Miss Wisconsin Jayme Dawicki, 2003, photo by David J. Marcou.

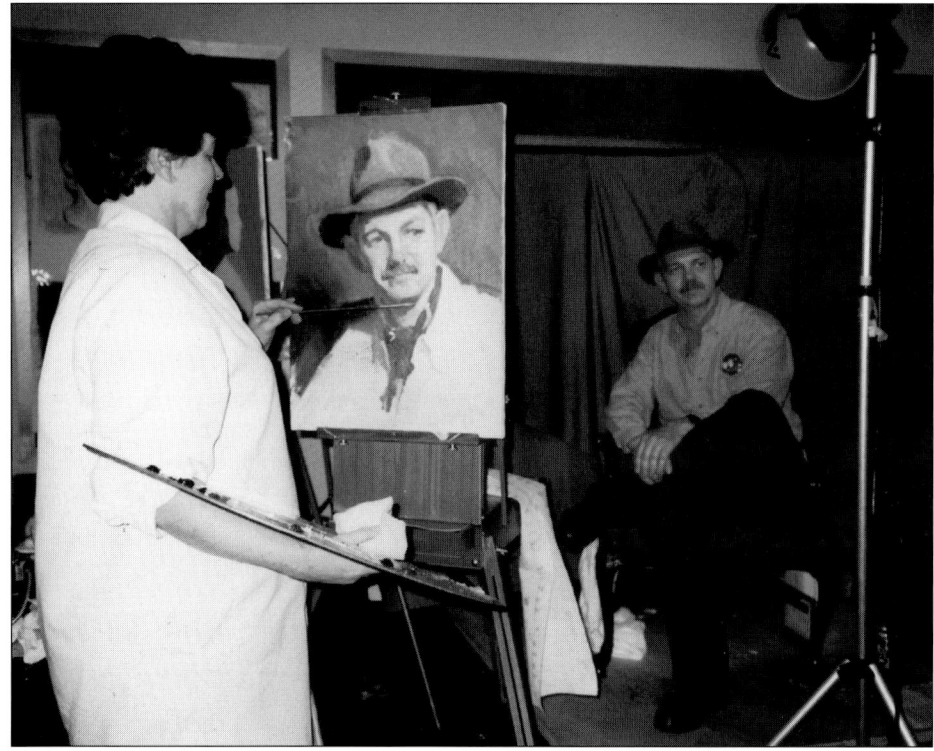

Peggy Baumgaertner painting a portrait of her husband, Jim, 2000, courtesy of Dr. James and Peggy Baumgaertner.

many informal, on-site portraits and scenes that resulted in groundbreaking labor reforms. He also photographed skyscraper builders up at the top, and has been called by Time Books (along with Jacob Riis) one of the two pillars of modern American photojournalism.

Edward Steichen fell in love with photography at age sixteen. A painter at an early age, he introduced the art of Rodin, Matisse, and Picasso to America. He directed photo units in two world wars and was chief photographer for *Vanity Fair* and *Vogue*. Among his subjects were Wisconsin natives Frank Lloyd Wright, Georgia O'Keeffe, and Orson Welles. Later, he became the first photography director of the Museum of Modern Art and curated the monumental Family of Man exhibition in 1955. When he died at age ninety-three, *The New York Times* called him America's "most celebrated and highest paid photographer."

La Crosse painter Peggy Baumgaertner respects traditional portraiture. A finalist in many national shows, she won Best of Show in the Portrait Society of America's 2000 National Competition for "The Charlton Family." Her portrait "Clare" was selected for the cover of *Best of Portraiture* (Northlights Books, 1997). Her commissions include Consulate of Malta Joseph Micallef, CEOs, Colin Powell, Tommy Thompson, the Beach Boys' Mike Love and Carl Wilson, and Drs. Edwin Overholt, Eugene Mayberry and Robert Waller. Her paintings hang in collections around the world.

Melvin Diemer operated a photo studio in Madison and was also staff photographer for the UW-Madison College of Agriculture and Home Economics Department. He made informal portraits of workers and students from 1900 to the 1930s. His informal portrait of Mr. and Mrs. Frank Lloyd Wright at Taliesin East graces the back cover of this book.

Portraits and Wisconsin 43

Best of Show for the 2000 National Conference of the Portrait Society of America, "The Charlton Family," original painting by Peggy Baumgaertner.

Badger cheerleaders by Lincoln statue and Bascom Hall, UW–Madison, circa 2004, courtesy of UW-Madison.

Athletes, Artists, and Workers

Steve Kiedrowski and David J. Marcou

Thomas Carlyle wrote, "Blessed is he who has found his work; let him ask no other blessing." Badger State denizens display a sound work ethic: we find our work and are blessed by it.

Athletes

The Green Bay Packers' Brett Favre overcame grief due to family deaths and his wife's cancer to turn in another stellar season in 2004. This Ironman/Huck Finn is the only NFL player to win three Most Valuable Player (MVP) awards. The only NFL team owned by its fans, the Packers have won the most league titles (12). Henry Aaron holds the major league baseball record for career home runs (755); and his teammate, pitcher Warren Spahn, holds the record for the most wins by a lefthander (363), even though he missed three seasons while on military duty. Aaron and Spahn played for the 1957 world champion Milwaukee Braves.

Tribute to UW footballer Ron Dayne (#33) when he broke the NCAA career rushing record, Camp Randall, Madison, 1999, photo by Gary Coorough.

Athletes, Artists, and Workers 45

Top: Brett Favre in practice-red jersey leads Packer offense vs. Packer defense, Green Bay, photo by Chuck Dockendorff.

Inset: Three Packer Super Bowl trophies, Lambeau Field offices, Green Bay, 2004, photo by John Wiatt.

Right: Packer quarterback Bart Starr (15) after diving for winning touchdown behind Jerry Kramer's (64) block vs. Dallas, 21–17, Green Bay, December 31, 1967, photo by John Biever (copyright © Vernon Biever).

UW-La Crosse sprinter Andrew Rock a few months before winning a gold medal at the 2004 Athens Olympics, photo by Bob Mulock.

Gale-Ettrick-Trempealeau High School's Coulee Region 2004 Lineman of the Year Andy Komperud, who died in a car crash just before he was to have learned of his award, courtesy of Steve Kiedrowski.

The Milwaukee Bucks' Kareem Abdul Jabbar led his team to an NBA title as scoring champ/MVP—then starred for Los Angeles's Lakers. University of Wisconsin system teams have won national titles, as have those of Marquette University; and UW-Madison footballer Ron Dayne broke the NCAA career rushing record in 1999. Madison's Eric Heiden won the Sullivan Award for five gold medals in the 1980 Olympics, where UW-Madison's Mark Johnson led the U.S. miracle hockey team. Dan Jansen, Paul Hamm, and Andrew Rock are also among Wisconsin's Olympic gold medalists. West Allis's Bonnie Blair was the most gilded American woman in Olympic history, with five golds. The first African American Olympic medalist, George Poage, graduated from La Crosse High School and UW-Madison, winning two bronzes at St. Louis's 1904 Olympics. And Cambridge's Matt Kenseth was a NASCAR driver of the year.

Artists

Film directors Nicholas Ray and Joseph Losey hailed from the Coulee Region. Ray directed James Dean in *Rebel without a Cause,* and Losey directed Richard Burton and Elizabeth Taylor in *Boom.*

Athletes, Artists, and Workers

Top left: 2002 La Crosse Aquinas High School boys' state championship basketball team, Madison, courtesy of Aquinas High School.

Top right: Manager Charlie Freiberg holds his team's championship softball trophy, Wausau, August 2004, photo by Chris Freiberg.

Below left: West Salem native Damian Miller's return to Wisconsin to lead the Milwaukee Brewers to the team's hoped-for championship status is one of the leading sports stories of 2005, courtesy of Steve Kiedrowski.

Below right: Winningest lefthanded pitcher ever, Milwaukee Braves' Warren Spahn, 1950s, photo by Milwaukee Journal Sentinel *for the Wisconsin Historical Society (ID#6224).*

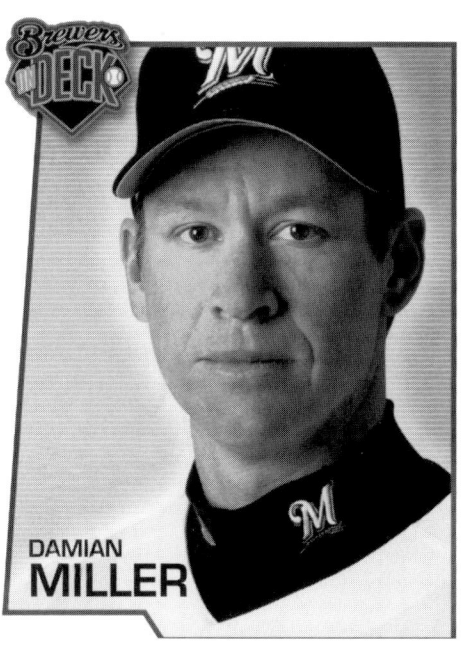

Trans-Wisconsin crew led by UW-Madison professor John Sharpless, which traced the Marquette-Joliet voyage of discovery along the Fox and Wisconsin Rivers from Lake Winnebago to Prairie du Chien, 2002, courtesy of Professor Sharpless.

Racine's Fredric March and Ellen Corby; Kenosha's Orson Welles and Don Ameche; Milwaukee's Spencer Tracy, Pat O'Brien, and Gene Wilder; Beaver Dam's Fred McMurray; Madison's Chris Farley, Brad Whitford, and his wife, Milwaukeean Jane Kaczmarek, became great actors. Welles starred in or directed many classic films, like *Citizen Kane* and the 1938 radio spoof that spooked a nation, *War of the Worlds,* about a Martian invasion. Beloved stage couple Lunt and Fontanne built their home, Ten Chimneys, at Genesee Depot; their friends included the Queen Mother, Helen Hayes, Katharine Hepburn, Noel Coward, the Redgraves, and Sir Laurence Olivier.

Other famed artists had state ties. Architect Frank Lloyd Wright was born in Richland Center and built Taliesin East near Spring Green. His Fallingwater House, Johnson Wax Building, Guggenheim Museum, Imperial Hotel, Monona Terrace, Usonian homes, and Unity Temple elevated all the arts. In photography, Milwaukee-raised Edward Steichen became the most famous portraitist of his era and directed the huge *Family of Man* exhibit in 1955 for New York's Museum of Modern Art (MOMA). Ashland's John Szarkowski, a UW-Madison graduate and superb photographer

Athletes, Artists, and Workers 49

Top: La Crosse Community Theatre Director Morrie Enders (L) instructs actors during rehearsal for It's a Wonderful Life, *2004, photo by Steve Kiedrowski.*

Middle: Mars (the "red planet" that inspired Orson Welles's and Steven Spielberg's renditions of H.G. Welles's War of the Worlds *and site of exploration by Rover "Spirit" and "Opportunity") and Moon, computer illustration by Mike Kiedrowski.*

Bottom: Cast and crew of Scott Thompson's film The Last Bridge Home, *2003, photo by David J. Marcou.*

Madison-born Thornton Wilder, three-time Pulitzer Prize winner, one for the classic drama Our Town, *photo for the Wisconsin Historical Society (ID #2655).*

himself, was Steichen's successor for twenty-nine years as MOMA's director of photography.

Madison-born Thornton Wilder won three Pulitzer Prizes for writing the plays *Our Town* and *Skin of Our Teeth* and the novel *Bridge of San Luis Rey*. West Salem's Hamlin Garland and La Crosse's John Toland were also among Pulitzer Prize-winners from Wisconsin, as were two female writers, Zona Gale for *Lulu Bett* and Edna Ferber for *So Big*. Portage-born Gale graduated from UW-Madison. Ferber was a teenager in Appleton and became a journalist and author. Many of her later novels and plays became movies, including *Show Boat, So Big, Dinner at Eight,* and *Giant,* with James Dean. UW-Madison's Esther M. Jackson wrote the first book-length critique of Tennessee Williams's plays. UW-Madison's Daniel T. Rodgers won the Frederick Jackson Turner Award for *The Work Ethic in Industrial America, 1850–1920*. Children's author Laura Ingalls Wilder was born near Lake Pepin, and author August Derleth was born and raised in Sauk City.

Sun Prairie-born Georgia O'Keeffe set high standards for modern painters with her wondrous flowers, cattle bones, crosses, and clouds. She'd been trained by nuns in Madison, and was unique. She married art impresario Alfred Stieglitz, the one man she couldn't win an argument with.

Magic-genius Harry Houdini was born in Hungary and came as a toddler to Appleton; his father was first rabbi there. Britain's *Daily Mirror* savaged West Allis-born pianist Wladziu Valentino Liberace, just short of calling him homosexual. His tiny court award elicited, "I cried all the way to the bank." Ko-Thi Dance director Ferne Caulker, a native of West Africa, inspired her group, based at UW-Milwaukee. Among hit TV series set here were *Happy Days,* with Ron Howard and Henry Winkler; *Laverne and Shirley,* with Penny Marshall and Cindy Williams; and *That '70s Show,* with Topher Grace and Ashton Kutcher. Others entertainers born or bred in Wisconsin include Agnes

Athletes, Artists, and Workers 51

Mr. and Mrs. Frank Lloyd Wright reading at home, Taliesin East, Spring Green, 1936, photo by Melvin E. Diemer for the Wisconsin Historical Society (ID#3976).

Former UW-Madison, now Princeton University Professor Daniel T. Rodgers, winner of the Frederick Jackson Turner Award for his book The Work Ethic in Industrial America, 1850–1920, *Madison, 1970s, courtesy of Professor Rodgers.*

Moorehead, Les Paul, Al Jarreau, Jerry Beck, Tom Wopat, Jerry and David Zucker, Willem Dafoe, Heather Graham, and Scott Thompson.

Workers

Wisconsin's workers have labored as hard, cursed as loud, laughed with and loved their families and colleagues as much as any workers anywhere—and in this book, readers will see many workers of one sort or another. Everyday public and private sector workers, entrepreneurs, and their companies have also helped Wisconsin to excel. Pabst, Miller, Heileman/City, and Schlitz breweries, J.I. Case, International Harvester, Harley-Davidson, Milwaukee Road, Sentry, Alan Bradley, Evinrude, Trane, Kohler, Kohl, IGA, Kwik Trip, and other big employers have been or are still strong in the state. Hi-tech companies and construction firms are advancing rapidly. And Wisconsin's small businesses show ingenuity and effort in producing quality goods and services at reasonable prices. All have much to do with Wisconsin's being a strong and diverse world leader.

Train, truck, and factory, Wausau, 1998, photo by David J. Marcou.

Athletes, Artists, and Workers 53

Blacksmith, Old World Wisconsin, historical restoration near Milwaukee, 1997, photo by Peg Jerome.

Above: Art table created by Galesville blacksmiths Patrick Nichols and Brad Nichols (no relation), courtesy of From Forge to Form, LLC.

Left: Standard Oil's La Crosse staff, 1920s, courtesy of James Grenisen.

Faith in Wisconsin

Fr. Bernard McGarty

Archeologists identify the Oneota as living near La Crosse and Lake Winnebago ten thousand years ago. Early artifacts at their tombs indicate they believed in life after death. Other pre-Columbian peoples who were here or eventually came here are identified as Potawatomi, Kickapoo, Ho-Chunk (Winnebago), Menominee, Ojibwe, Mohican, Oneida, Brothertown, Sioux, Sac, and

Congregation Sons of Abrham Synagogue, La Crosse, 2005, photo by Robert Joseph.

Cathedral interior, La Crosse, circa 2000, photo by Debbie Abraham.

Fathers Roger Scheckel, Joe Walijewski, and Sebastian Kolodziejczyk, courtesy of Father Scheckel. Fathers Walijewski and Kolodziejczyk operate an orphanage sponsored by the La Crosse Diocese, Casa Hogar Juan Pablo II, in Lurin, Peru, near Lima.

Fox, recognizing a Great Spirit, Manitou, corresponding to the European God. Manitou—creator of the gifts of land, sky, sun, moon, and water—produces life and growth. Dance and chant still are liturgical forms. A tall pole with maize at the top is traditionally offered to Manitou.

The French period, 1634–1763, began when Jean Nicolet, dressed as a mandarin expecting to find China, landed at Red Banks near today's Green Bay. Catholic missionaries followed—Jesuits Rene Menard, Claude Allouez, and Jacques Marquette, who catechized the natives and named the Apostle Islands, Madeline Island, La Pointe, and the Bay of the Holy Spirit (Chequamegon Bay).

Most early European explorers and fur traders were Catholic, like Nicholas Perrot, Pierre-Esprit Radisson, and Medart Chouart des Groseilliers. Churches were erected at La Pointe, Green Bay, and Prairie du Chien, serving French and natives. Father Louis Hennepin, OFM, skirted western Wisconsin as his group traveled the Mississippi until their capture at Lake Pepin.

British domination, 1763–1815, followed the French defeat at Quebec. Captain Jonathan Carver took control of the western Wisconsin area. Fox and Indian wars inhibited settlement and there were no Catholic clergy after 1728 for one hundred years. The Church of England became the established religion until the Revolution; the established religion after that was Episcopalianism. The U.S. Constitution established freedom of religion, accommodating a variety of missionary

Faith in Wisconsin   57

Above: The Flying Nun *actress Sally Field and friends in the TV series inspired by Wisconsin novelist Tere Rios Versace's book* The Fifteenth Pelican, *photo by ABC Press Information for the Wisconsin Historical Society (ID #11051).*

Below: Father Roger Scheckel places flowers on the tomb of Blessed Mother Teresa during his tour of an Indian parish sponsored by his church, Calcutta, India, 2004, courtesy of Father Scheckel.

Right: Paul Granlund's "Damascus Illumination," St. Paul's Lutheran Church, La Crosse, 2005, photo by Robert Joseph.

societies from Eastern states. Foremost were the Congregational, Presbyterian, Methodist, Baptist, and Episcopal.

After the Wisconsin area was taken over from Britain in 1815, and after statehood in 1848, the number of religions increased. The 1850 census listed 365 Wisconsin churches—including 110 Methodist, 64 Roman Catholic, 49 Baptist, 40 Presbyterian, 37 Congregational, 20 Lutheran, 19 Episcopal, 6 Universalist, 4 Christian, 2 Dutch Reformed, 1 Union and 11 other sects. Rock County had the most, 52, and Milwaukee 38. The general population was 305,391. Immigrants from Germany were Catholic and Lutheran; from Wales, Methodist; from Ireland, Catholic; from Scandinavia, Lutheran; from New England, Episcopal, Methodist, Presbyterian, and Congregational. Mormons going west settled briefly near La Crosse and Black River Falls. Mainline Christian Churches did not preach much against slavery before the Civil War, unlike Universalists and Quakers.

Above: Exterior of the Chapel of Mary of the Angels seen from the air, St. Rose Convent, photo by Carl Liebig.

Right: Stairway spiral of the Melk (Austria) Abbey, a former base of operations for the La Crosse Boychoir, photo by Professor Roger Grant.

Faith in Wisconsin   59

Left: Raymond L. Burke, former La Crosse bishop and new St. Louis archbishop, receives the pallium from Pope John Paul II, the Vatican, June 29, 2004, L'Osservatore Romano *via* Father Roger Scheckel.

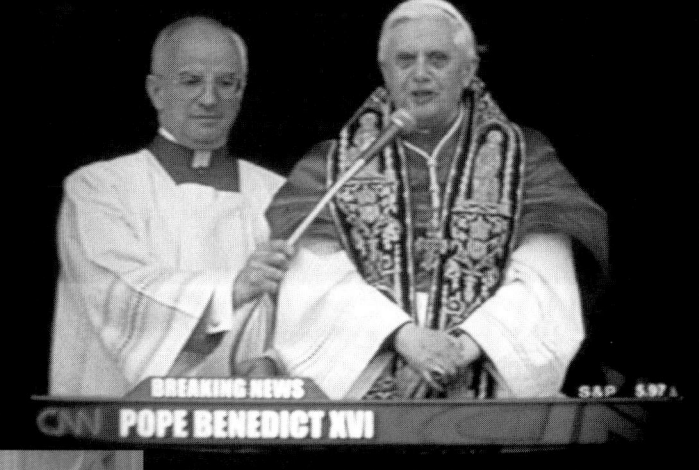

Right: Pope Benedict XVI addresses the crowd the day of his election, Rome, June 20, 2005, retrieved from television in Wisconsin.

Left: New La Crosse Diocesan Bishop Jerome Listecki entering from the Cathedral vestibule for his installation, La Crosse, March 1, 2005, photo by David J. Marcou.

Right: Drs. Robert and Carole Edland meet John Paul II. Carole is a Rite of Christian Initiation Director in western Wisconsin and Director of the Butterfly Ministry, a grief support group. 1995, courtesy of the Edlands.

Cancer patient Devyn Marie Doughty with her puppy, Chelsea, a few months before Devyn passed away, Eau Claire, 2001, courtesy of her maternal grandparents, Drs. Robert and Carole Edland.

The Swiss, Dutch and Belgians came to Wisconsin in discrete numbers with specialized trades and were Evangelical, Lutheran, Baptist, or Catholic. Industrial jobs and farming attracted Poles, Bohemians, French Canadians, and Austrians, who were largely Catholic. By 1880, 30 percent of the population was foreign-born. Blacks and Baptists were in the minority, as were Jews. By 1900 the population of Wisconsin was 2,069,042.

In the twentieth century, mainline Christianity was augmented by Seventh Day Adventist, Salvation Army, Pentecostal and Disciples of Christ denominations. Then, in 1956, Congress opened immigration to people from the Middle East and Asia. In 2001 there were 7 million Muslims in the country, with 7,798 in Wisconsin. The Amish began buying state farmland in 1960. Today there are about 12,000 here. Jews have worshiped in Wisconsin for two centuries; their number now is 28,230.

Every community in Wisconsin is enriched by church architecture that includes Colonial, Greek Revival, Romanesque, Victorian, Gothic, Prairie, Spanish, Oriental, Eastern, and more modern styles.

Education is also integral. Nashota House is a nationally recognized Episcopal seminary. Concordia and Carthage colleges are prestigious Lutheran institutions. There are sixteen church-sponsored colleges and universities in Wisconsin, with Marquette University (Jesuit), having the largest enrollment (7,775). About 145,000 students attend religious/independent primary and secondary schools, or one of every four students.

Social services include hospitals, of which thirty-six are operated by church bodies. Nursing homes and self-care units are operated by the Seventh Day Adventists and other mainline faiths. All churches reach out to the poor. Many offer counseling, adoption services, and halfway houses.

The civil rights movement of the 1960s saw Father James Groppi in Milwaukee lead marches for fair housing. Most churches fought discrimination, following Martin Luther King's lead. He visited the state several times then. The morality of the Vietnam and Iraq wars is questioned by individual clergy and laity and by the Quakers.

A state report in 2000 listed sixty-one religious bodies in 4,841 congregations with a total of 3,191,834 adherents. The state population in 2005 is about 5,472,000. If statistics are true, more than half of Wisconsin's residents participate in religion, compared to one-third in 1850.

Above left: The Rev. Canon Patrick Augustine, candlelit peace ceremony, Christ Episcopal Church, La Crosse, photo by Professor Roger Grant.

Above right: Wheelchair madonna and child, St. Joseph the Workman Cathedral, 2003–04, photo by David J. Marcou.

Left: Amish wool socks on clothesline, Vernon County, 2004, photo by Professor Roger Grant.

Below: Frank Lloyd Wright's First Unitarian Church, Madison, photo by Donald Sylvester.

Wisconsinites Who Serve

La Crosse Police Lieutenant Daniel J. Marcou

Half-staff sunrise service, French Island Cemetery, Memorial Day, 2004, courtesy of James Grenisen.

The common definitions for "service" fall short of quantifying the dedication, devotion, and bravery of Wisconsinites who serve the public. They are Heroes.

At eighteen, Arthur MacArthur enlisted in Milwaukee to save the Union and end slavery. He was a first lieutenant in the 24th Wisconsin Regiment, and on November 25, 1863, General Grant's Army was under siege in Chattanooga. Grant ordered troops to take the Confederate rifle pits at the base of Missionary Ridge. This assault was a feint to aid General Sherman's faltering main assault.

Civil War honorable discharge papers of Charles Zietlow, courtesy of the Don and LaVonne Zietlow Family.

A Wisconsin regiment of the famed Iron Brigade, known as the "Black Hats" for obvious reasons, Virginia, September, 1862, photo by Matthew Brady for the Wisconsin Historical Society (ID #4978).

Marine Robert Emmett Dwyer, who served loyally in the Pacific Theatre with Carlson's Raiders, June 6, 1944, courtesy of Sean Dwyer.

Troops including the 24th Wisconsin took the pits after a bitter fight, but then they were blasted by cannon fire from atop Missionary Ridge.

Without orders, the men launched an assault on the nearly impregnable heights. MacArthur saw a flag bearer killed by bayonet and a second decapitated by cannon ball. He picked up the flag and advanced, shouting, "On Wisconsin!" and led the charge up Missionary Ridge. When he reached the top, he firmly planted the flag. He infused spirit into the charge; the day was won. MacArthur won the Congressional Medal of Honor for his actions and eventually retired from the Army a general. He raised a son who also won the Medal of Honor—Gen. Douglas MacArthur (http://www.homeofheroes.com/hallofheroes/1st_floor/flag/1bf_mac.html).

During World War II, Poplar, Wisconsin's Richard Ira (Joe) Bong became the most successful fighter pilot in American history. He flew two hundred combat missions, shooting down forty Japanese planes and many enemy troops and sinking several ships. Bong died testing a new jet—a P–80—the same day the A-bomb fell on Hiroshima. A journalist-witness said Bong could have parachuted early and lived but held onto the controls longer to avoid hitting homes.

Before Joe Bong's time in the service, Milwaukee pilot Billy Mitchell was top ace in World War I. Later, as a general, he tried to persuade authorities that future wars depended on airpower. His warning was not heeded, and lack of air power proved deadly when Japanese planes overwhelmed U.S. air and sea forces at Pearl Harbor. By

Les and Ann Olson on their wedding day, Granada, Mississippi, June 10, 1944, courtesy of Dan and Vicki Marcou.

General MacArthur at presentation of Congressional Medal of Honor to Poplar, Wisconsin's very own all-time No. 1 U.S. flying ace, Richard Bong, The Philippines, December 12, 1944, U.S. Signal Corps for the Wisconsin Historical Society (ID#11076).

Vietnam vets on parade, western Wisconcin, circa 2000, photo by David J. Marcou.

World War II's end, though, U.S. airpower had won. Today, General Mitchell International Airport in Milwaukee is named for this warrior-seer.

Wisconsin's own have served in all branches since 1848. Private Lester A. Olson, of West Salem, fought his way across Europe in Patton's Third Army. Marine Robert E. Dwyer, of La Crosse, went on the "Long Patrol" behind Japanese lines at Guadalcanal with Carlson's Raiders. A general's stories are written in ink, a soldier's in blood.

In Korea, two western Wisconsin soldiers fought especially valiantly, killing many enemy before being killed themselves—Cpl. Mitchell Red Cloud, a Hatfield Ho-Chunk who had also served in Carlson's Raiders in World War II, and Mindoro's Pfc. Stanley R. Christianson were posthumously awarded the Congressional Medal of Honor. They were brave and able, as was Marine Cpl. Frank Devine, of La Crosse, who won the Silver Star at Seoul.

Many also serve bravely at home. Police officers give their all 24-7 for little pay or respect. On November 24, 1917, Officers Fred Kaiser, David Obrien, Paul Weiler, Albert Templin, Charles Seehawk, Frank Laswin, Steven Stecher, Henry Deckert, and Edward Spindler of the Milwaukee Police Department died when a package a boy dropped off at the department's central precinct blew

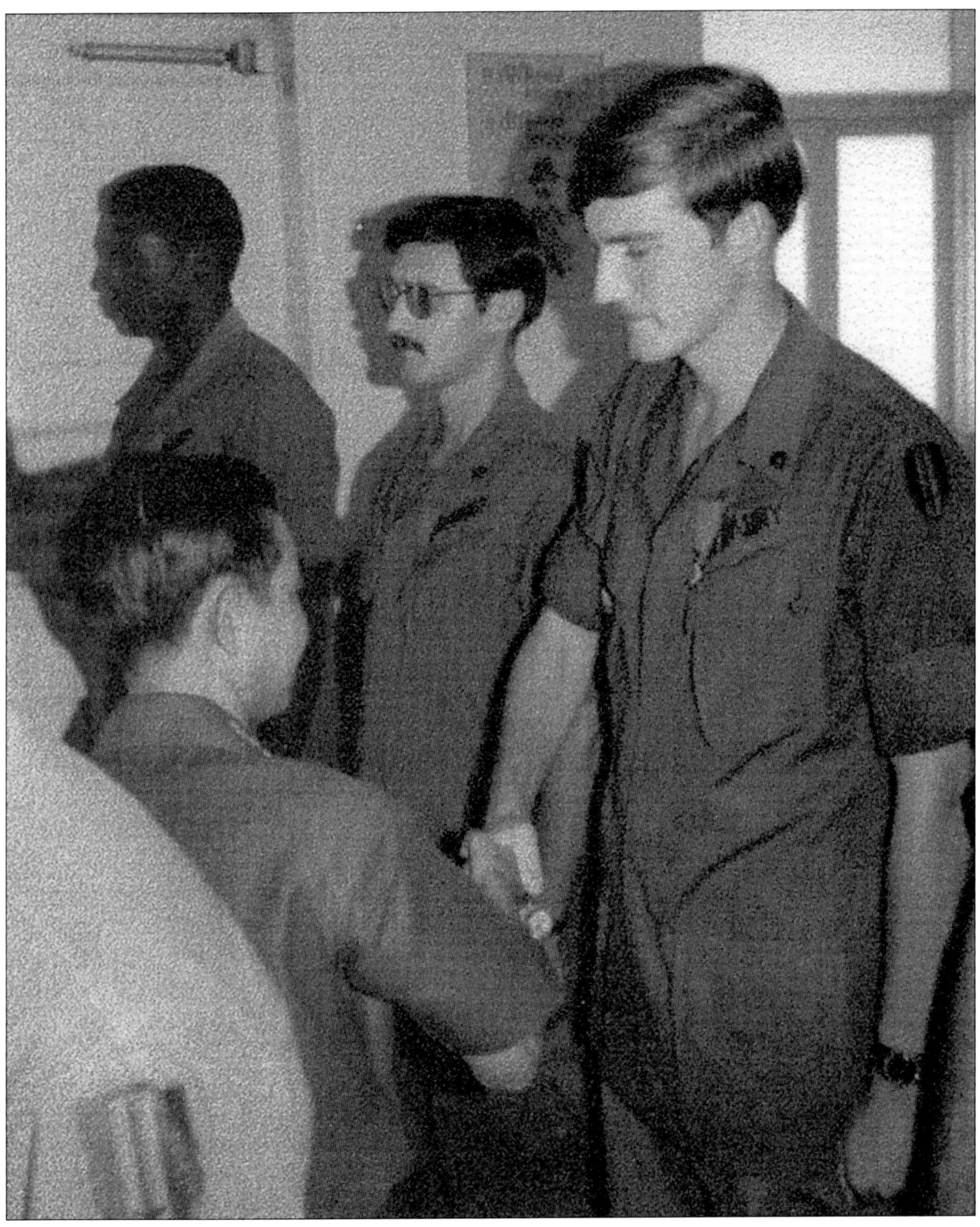

Trooper John Satory receives the Vietnam Service Medal, Vietnam, early 1970s, courtesy of the John and Beth Satory Family.

Police officer Joseph Donndelinger's funeral after he was shot and killed in the line of duty, old St. Joseph's Cathedral, December 1937, courtesy of the La Crosse Police Department.

up. Anarchists were to blame. It was the worst day for police in state history, and it is the only time in U.S. history that a police dispatcher has been killed in the line of duty.

Firefighters serve, too. From battling the largest, deadliest forest fire in North American history—the Peshtigo Fire of October 8, 1871 (which killed more than a thousand people, far more than the Great Chicago Fire that occurred the same day)—to fighting fires today with better equipment, techniques, and pay, dangers still exist and firefighters face and overcome them daily.

And politicians serve, too. Mayor Wilson Colwell, of La Crosse, served very well. He could have been in City Hall the day he died, but on September 14, 1862, Captain Colwell led his La Crosse boys up South Mountain and was killed by a rebel bullet. That day, Colwell's brigade earned the sobriquet "The Iron Brigade." His regiment returned home physically depleted but spiritually undiminished. These best, bravest riflemen of the Army suffered the highest killed-in-action ratio of any Union regiment, but the Iron Brigade was proud that it always moved forward and never took a step backward in battle unless ordered. (Note that our state motto is "Forward.")

Firefighters with their hoses at the Oscar's Restaurant fire, Onalaska, 1988, photo by the La Crosse Tribune *via the Terry and Cheryl Smith Family.*

La Crosse Police SWAT unit, City Hall, 2003, courtesy of the La Crosse Police Department. Lieutenant/Training Officer Dan Marcou, co-recipient with an Oak Creek officer of the 2004 Wisconsin SWAT Officer of the Year Award for his work preventing further killing by a hostage-taker, and author of two histories of the department, is third from left in front next to Police Chief Edward Kondracki (center front).

Top: Wisconsin native Army Special Forces trooper Chad Miller, Afghanistan, 2004, courtesy of Cory Miller.

Bottom: Wisconsin native Private/Medic Michelle Witmer, courtesy of the official Michelle Witmer memorial website.

Other brave men and women have worked in the Peace Corps, VISTA, Americorps, and other nonmilitary service organizations. Governor Jim Doyle—and his wife, Jessica, both of whom sprang from famous Wisconsin political families—served in Tunisia in the Peace Corps after graduating from UW-Madison and then worked on a Navajo Indian reservation in Chinle, Arizona, after graduating from Harvard Law School. Governor Doyle has served Wisconsin well in-state for more than twenty years since; Jessica Doyle has been a dedicated teacher during that time. And it would be imprudent not to mention "Fighting Bob" LaFollette, whose very nickname and life epitomized the spirit of Wisconsin, though he opposed U.S. involvement in World War I, a war whose uneasy treaty led to World War II.

Recently, a guardswoman joined the ranks of those who have served from Wisconsin and paid the ultimate price. Private/Medic Michelle Witmer, of New Berlin, and her two sisters served well in the Iraq War. Michelle died in an enemy attack on Baghdad on April 9, 2004. She served with the National Guard's 32nd Military Police Company and was the first female National Guard soldier in the nation ever to be killed in combat as well as the first Wisconsin National Guard soldier killed in combat since World War II. She is missed, along with all of the other troopers from Wisconsin who have given their lives for freedom.

The next time you hear "On Wisconsin!" sung at a Badger game, take the time to remember—there was a moment when many good men and women from Wisconsin, boys and girls at heart with big dreams, were serving their state and country when those were the last words they heard.

Wisconsinites Who Serve 71

Pfc. Jon Kuehl of Brown Deer is with the 2nd Marine Division, 7th Battalion. His pictures were taken in Iraq from March to September, 2004. His base was on the outskirts of Baghdad, so the scenes are from that area.

Sunset over Iraq, 2004, photo by Jon Kuehl, USMC.

Communities and Families

tamara Horstman-Riphahn and Ronald S. Rochon, Ph.D.

Whether it's Friday night fish at a supper club in Barre Mills, fresh vegetable-filled spring rolls at a Hmong New Year celebration in Appleton, a brat with kraut steaming into the chill of Oktoberfest in La Crosse or Milwaukee, lefse-wrapped meatballs on a checkered tablecloth in Osseo, cheese curds at a pub in Green Bay, a walnut burger or catfish along the Mississippi River in Trempealeau, or a jumbled plate of spicy Somali curry chicken with lentils and rice on Capitol Square, one force brings strangers, families, neighbors, friends, colleagues, and communities together, and that is food.

No matter what our backgrounds are, the substances that we each choose to nourish our bodies serve as a vital representation of ourselves and our ancestors. No matter who we are, where we are from, or what our occupation is, each of us has a richness within and a recipe to offer. And when we come together to share our sustenance, in turn we share history, family, culture, and we build Wisconsin.

In the shadow of national and international tragedy and war, it would

Schubert's ice cream parlor and café, Mt. Horeb, 2004, photo by tamara Horstman-Riphahn.

Left: Four generations of Wisconsin females, circa 1900, courtesy of the Werner and Jolene Engel Family.

Below: Anna and Joe Motivans, Latvian-American couple, western Wisconsin, 1981, courtesy of Anna Motivans.

John Medinger's family early on, 1930s, courtesy of the John and Dee Medinger Family.

be easy to close our doors, barricade state lines, and foster suspicions of the "other." However, it's essential that even through the most difficult times, Wisconsinites continue to assist one another and contemplate our individual and local influence, strength, and responsibility to one another—what we can do and must do. Many times we strive to support and nurture those to whom we feel devoted, but in order to survive in the existing interdependent structure of our societies, we must also contemplate the ways in which we open our lives and provide opportunities for old and new alike.

Considering the future of Wisconsin communities, we must keep at the forefront of our minds what we want for our children. Our example teaches children what treatment they should expect and what actions they should perform. If we mock those we consider different, if we pollute our forests and rivers, or if we expect instant fulfillment of our wants, our children will repeat our examples—and far too often, will repeat our mistakes. However, if we offer eye contact with a genuine "How are you?" to those who serve, assist, and clean up after us, if we explore the distinction of local flora, or if we invite a family from "across the tracks" to enjoy a meal, our children will also replicate these examples, and traditions of generosity and compassion will develop.

Wisconsin has a history of valuing the ideals of enrichment and welcome. However, infused in these ideals is the principle of deliberative democratic dialogue. Wisconsin citizens have struggled

Communities and Families

Above: Children in circle, photo by tamara Horstman-Riphan.

Left: Ron and Lynn Rochon's daughter and son, Nia and Ayinda, Onalaska, 2002, photo by Ronald S. Rochon.

Below: tamara and Peter Horstman-Riphahn's wedding party, West Salem, 2004, photo by Shelly Horstman.

Zita and Ed Pretasky on their golden anniversary, La Crosse, 2004, photo by Mary (Pretasky) Burke.

with the complexity of multiple positions on a host of issues, including assisting escaped African slaves through the Underground Railroad, welcoming Hmong refugees from repressive camps in Laos and Thailand, and debating the ethics of using Native American imagery for school mascots. During these historical struggles, many Wisconsin citizens have offered comfort and sustenance. These individuals understand and believe that it is through the inclusion of all voices that growth, responsibility, and enrichment will occur. Through the process of difficult dialogues and the welcoming of "outsiders," the state of Wisconsin will continue to grow stronger and become a better state for *all* of its citizens.

If we consider communities and families within Wisconsin, we will recognize that it is through our encounters that we begin to understand the richness of varying experiences and cultures, histories and dreams, sacrifices and celebrations. It is during times of shared meals and extensive conversation that people connect to established as well as newly arrived residents. When we extend an invitation to a new colleague, neighbor, or classmate to join our friends and families for a meal, we are in essence opening avenues for relationships and supportive bonds to develop. And when we present these invitations to "strangers," we are helping to build a new Wisconsin—a stronger Wisconsin. We break down barriers, we eradicate fear, and most significantly, we teach our children about

Communities and Families 77

Left: Cousins Joe (L) and Matt Marcou, Myrick Park, La Crosse, circa 1999, photo by David J. Marcou.

Below: Zietlow Family Christmas card, 2004, courtesy of the Don and LaVonne Zietlow Family.

the importance of sharing, accepting, and community building. When we rely on each other, we become more than just a collection of individuals involved in individual endeavors; rather, we truly become a community.

Over blemished oak family tables passed on through generations, slightly wobbly restaurant tables cloaked in linen, café countertops littered with condiments, or faded picnic tables etched with lovers' names, we come together to gossip, debate, laugh, and learn while we eat. It is while breaking bread that community members build an understanding of the beauty in our individual distinctiveness and learn to recognize the human spirit within one another.

Nancy's grandson Dietrick, West Salem, circa 1997, photo by Nancy Horstman.

Top left: The Dirk and Shiela Slaback Family in a tree fort, western Wisconsin, 2004, photo by Laurie Reed.

Top right: Maid-Rite café next to Sweet Shop, La Crosse, 2003, photo by tamara Horstman-Riphahn.

Left: Tim and Kati Freiberg with cousin Jon Kuehl (center), Brown Deer, October 2004, photo by Chris Freiberg.

Wisconsin in La Crosse

Anita Taylor Doering

Nestled along the eastern shore of the Mississippi River, La Crosse was built upon a sand prairie guarded on the east by bluffs—a gift of the Driftless Area during the Ice Age. The unglaciated area became known as the Coulee Region (*coulee* meaning valley). Early French explorers traveled the Mississippi and labeled the site where the Mississippi, Black, and La Crosse rivers converge as Prairie á la Crosse. As legend has it, the explorers observed native peoples, probably Ho-Chunk (Winnebago), playing a field game that reminded them of the French game of lacrosse. While the locale was not a permanent settlement for Native Americans, it was a meeting ground and thought to be used occasionally as a campsite.

Lacrosse Players statue by Elmer Petersen and clock, Main Street, photo by Dr. Carole Edland.

Boat and houseboats, Black River, six-part join-up photo by Bob Mulock.

Delta Queen *moored near two bridges, Mississippi River, 2004, photo by Sam McKay.*

Police horse, photo by Mark Smith.

After the defeat of the Sauk and Fox native peoples in the Black Hawk War of 1832, the land that included western Wisconsin was cleared for white settlement. Nathan Myrick, considered to be the first permanent white settler in La Crosse and its first postmaster, shortened Prairie á la Crosse to simply La Crosse. Myrick and his first partner, Eben Weld, began a fur-trading post on Barron's Island in 1841. The next year, young Myrick and a new partner, Harmon J. B. Miller, moved their trading post across river to the site of present-day La Crosse. Trade was brisk in muskrat, raccoon, mink, and other furs and silver coins for goods.

In 1836 Wisconsin's territorial boundaries were formed from Michigan Territory, and in 1848 Wisconsin became the thirtieth state, when La Crosse was still an infant. Early in the 1850s, Yankees—British-American migrants from the East Coast—began to come west and settle in the pioneer state of Wisconsin. European immigrants from Germany, Norway, France, Switzerland, Bohemia, and other countries followed in turn. Many of the Yankees pressed on farther west, but not before the city of La Crosse had been chartered in 1856 by the state legislature. La Crosse experienced rapid growth in the nineteenth century as a center of commerce and a place to distribute goods.

Agriculture and lumber were the two mainstays of the economy in the nineteenth century. Most immigrants wanted their own land to farm but needed cash quickly. The pioneers soon learned to

Top: La Crosse Loggers baseball game, photo by Paul Abraham.

Right: Recovery Room 1992 city champion softball team, courtesy of Dennis A. Marcou.

Left: *Former State Assemblyman and Mayor John Medinger at Hmong New Year's celebration, courtesy of the John and Dee Medinger Family.*

Right: *Bicyclist at WKBT-Channel 8 TV, 2005, photo by David J. Marcou.*

squelch prairie fires to protect their property, and row crops and livestock took the place of grasslands and prairie chickens. Oxen were the work animals of choice initially. Dairy farming caught on after William Hoard published *Hoard's Dairyman* and promoted dairy farming in the state. Wheat was the cash crop of the 1860s, but it soon gave way to hay, oats, and corn, as they were used to feed livestock. (Wheat also depleted the ground of nutrients and made the land useless if proper crop rotation was not practiced.)

La Crosse served as the outlet for giant pine logs that were timbered from the Black River forests and floated downriver. Already in 1848, Myrick had counted eleven sawmills along the Black River. Major mills were located along the Mississippi River in La Crosse, which fueled the pocketbooks of many former New Englanders. By 1890, the city's population had grown to second highest in the state, after Milwaukee. When the lumber supply was exhausted around 1900, the lumber barons moved west or south. Agriculture kept the area going, though physical growth in the city stalled.

Top: Doc Powell's building/corner, as seen in 1887, is now in the Historic Downtown District, courtesy of La Crosse Public Library Archives.

Right: Then-Mayor John Medinger (seated left) and other principals in Jazz on the Green's Causeway *group, courtesy of the John and Dee Medinger Family.*

From left: Writer/archivist Anita T. Doering, Historical Society president George Italiano, State School Superintendent Elizabeth Burmaster, and library patron Richard Dungar, La Crosse Public Library, March 20, 2005, photo by David J. Marcou.

Breweries became a key type of business here, especially G. Heileman's (today's City Brewery), and eventually more companies began producing new products, like La Crosse Rubber Mills and La Crosse Plow Works. By the outbreak of World War II, the Electric Auto Lite Company, Trane Company, Northern Engraving, and other companies had garnered government contracts to help U.S. armed forces succeed. Eventually industry began to wane despite efforts by the city to develop industrial parks nearer to transportation corridors and away from the downtown area.

Since the 1970s, however, with its large urban renewal projects, La Crosse's commercial growth has again changed. Like many other cities, its economy has turned away from industrial production and it has become a service and technology center. The growth of the universities and technical college, as well as consolidation and growth of the area hospitals, has led education and health-care leaders into vital relationships, and La Crosse has become a destination for post-secondary students. And instead of new immigrants to La Crosse speaking Norwegian or German, today they often speak Hmong. There is renewed interest in historic preservation, neighborhoods, and community

Restored auto's Pearl Street reflections, photo by John J. Satory Jr.

Giant City Brewery/La Crosse Lager 6-pack, 2003, photo by Robert Joseph.

involvement. People are energized by community projects, such as Rotary Lights, the Skyrockers' New Year's Eve fireworks shows, Riverside Park Friendship Gardens, and Sister City relationships with Dubna, Russia; Epinal, France; Luoyang, China; Bantry, Ireland; and Friedberg, Germany. City universities continue to bring diversity and cultural events to La Crosse and its people.

Left: Ryan and Andy Kiedrowski with Milwaukee Brewers announcer Darren Sutton, 2005, photo by Steve Kiedrowski.

Below left: Mark Johnsrud is sworn in as mayor by City Clerk Teri Lehrke, April 2005, photo by Larry Lebiecki.

Below right: Grandad Bluff, photo by Dave Larsen.

Wisconsin in America

Roberta Stevens

Governor John Reynolds, President John F. Kennedy, and Earth Day founder, governor, and senator Gaylord Nelson, Apostle Islands, early 1960s, courtesy of Mr. and Mrs. Gaylord Nelson, the Wilderness Society, and the UW Alumni Association.

Wisconsin was one of the first areas in the Middle West to be visited by European explorers and fur traders from France, Spain, and England. When Frenchman Jean Nicolet landed on the Green Bay shores in 1634, he found a wilderness of trees, rivers, streams, and Native Americans. Early French explorers noted that the native word for the principal river was "Ouisconsin." The name probably comes from a Chippewa word translated as "gathering of waters." Thus did the area that would become the state of Wisconsin get its name.

Wisconsin in America 91

Onalaska's Roberta Stevens and former Atlanta Mayor/U.N. Ambassador Andrew Young, NAACP Convention, Rochester, Minnesota, circa 1989, courtesy of the Dr. Mark and Roberta Stevens Family.

Mayor John Medinger (third from left) and Congressman Ron Kind (right) with President Bill Clinton and entourage, January 1998, courtesy of the John and Dee Medinger Family.

NBC's Katie Couric and Whitehall's Mrs. Calista (Newt) Gingrich, courtesy of the Werner and Jolene Engel Family.

The Wisconsin area was under French control from 1634 to 1763, until it was won by the British. It was ceded to the United States by the Treaty of Paris in 1783, but it wasn't until after the War of 1812 that Americans had a real presence there. Treaties with the Native Americans from 1829 to 1833 opened up the state, but immigration was held up briefly during the Black Hawk War of 1832. This area became part of the Wisconsin Territory (formerly the Northwest, Indiana, and Michigan Territories) in 1836, and on May 29, 1848, President James K. Polk signed the bill making Wisconsin the thirtieth state in the Union. In 1837, Madison (then a town on paper), was selected as seat of Wisconsin's government and the first brick was laid for the Capitol building.

In the early 1800s, when most of the state was still Indian land, white settlers came to the lead mining areas of southwestern Wisconsin. Many of these settlers were New Englanders, Southerners, and immigrants of almost every European nationality, with Germans most numerous, followed by Poles, Norwegians, British and Swedes. There were smaller groups who came from southern Europe, the Netherlands, Belgium, French-Canada, Finland, and Switzerland. They were mainly Lutherans, Roman Catholics, and non-Lutheran Protestants.

During the Civil War (1861–65), Wisconsin furnished 52 regiments of infantry to defend the Union against the South. They comprised about 92,000 soldiers, including 79,934 volunteers, 11,445 drafted men and substitutes, 130 sailors, and 165 black men for the Negro regiments. Some of the more famous regiments were the 2nd, 6th, and 7th Wisconsin of the Iron Brigade. The 2nd Wisconsin Volunteer Infantry sustained the greatest percentage of losses (killed and died of wounds)

Boat Cave, Wisconsin Dells, photo by H.H. Bennett for the Wisconsin Historical Society (ID#7566).

Margaret Kiedrowski (later Brom) and then husband, Art Kiedrowski, Trempealeau County, courtesy of Steve Kiedrowski.

of any of the 2,000 regiments in the entire Union Army. At Gettysburg, it lost 77 percent of those engaged in battle, though it played a key role on the first day of battle.

A Wisconsinite who made a national reputation for himself early on was Robert "Fighting Bob" La Follette Sr., a governor of Wisconsin (1901–06) and U.S. Senator (1906–25) noted for his support of reform. The Progressive Party he organized was a short-lived independent political group assembled for the 1924 presidential election due to dissatisfaction with the conservative attitudes and programs of both Democrats and Republicans. The Progressive Party chose La Follette as its presidential candidate. The 1924 Progressives pledged a "housecleaning" of executive departments, public control of natural resources, public ownership of railways, and tax reduction. President Calvin Coolidge and the Republicans won the election. The Progressive Party dissolved when La Follette died in 1925.

Led by the La Follette family—including also Bob's wife Belle and sons Robert Jr. and Phillip—Wisconsin pioneered worker's compensation, vocational education, unemployment compensation, and state income taxes. More recently, several Wisconsin governors and senators have made national names for themselves. From the McCarthyism of disrespected Senator Joe McCarthy and the wry Golden Fleece Awards of Senator William Proxmire, McCarthy's more humane successor, to ambassador and cabinet appointments for contemporary politicians, Wisconsin has often appeared in the national spotlight.

The nickname "Badger State" comes from Wisconsin's lead miners. They were called "badgers"; as they reached a new site, they dug into the hillsides, much as badgers dig their burrows, and lived underground. Another Wisconsin nickname is "Copper State," referring to its northern copper mines.

"America's Dairyland" (yet another state nickname) has been a leader in producing milk and milk products since cheese factories multiplied in the latter part of the nineteenth century. Wisconsin's economy had been based on wheat until soil became depleted, among many problems, and farmers turned to dairy farming. Wisconsin cheese is now a very popular national and international delicacy. Also, the state leads the nation in sweet corn processing and is one of the top two states in cranberry production. About half the state's land is used as farmland. Wisconsin is also among the leaders in manufacturing machinery, turbines, and engines. Fifteen million acres of forests here are strictly conserved to ensure a steady lumber supply and natural beauty.

*TransAfrica founder/*Defending the Spirit *author Randall Robinson and Roberta Stevens, NAACP National Convention, Washington, D.C., 1988, courtesy of the Dr. Mark and Roberta Stevens Family.*

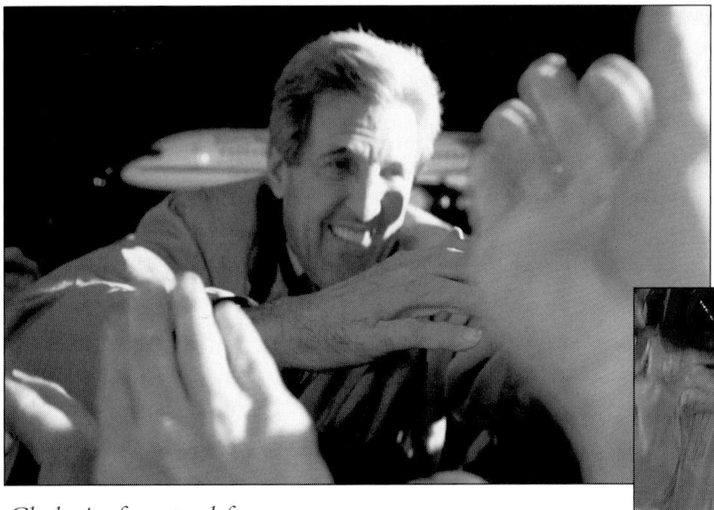

Clockwise from top left:
- *Senator Kerry works the crowd in front of the flag, La Crosse, Election Day, photo by Professor Roger Grant.*
- *Wisconsin votes, November 2, 2004, photo by David J. Marcou.*
- *Nick Coorough and actress Natalie Portman at Kerry rally, Madison, 2004, courtesy of Nick Coorough.*
- *Senator Kerry shakes hands, Election Day, photo by Professor Roger Grant.*

Wisconsin in America 97

Both major presidential candidates visited Wisconsin often before the 2004 election. The Badger State was pleased to meet both men, their families, friends, and many celebrities. President Bush visited the La Crosse area in May and October, and Senator Kerry visited the area in July and on election day. The President won reelection by three percentage points, while Senator Kerry took Wisconsin.

Clockwise from top:
- *President Bush schmoozes with a fan, May 2004, photo by David J. Marcou.*
- *President Bush's daughters appear during a state visit, November 1, 2004, photo by David J. Marcou.*
- *Laura Bush speaks before a crowd in La Crosse, photo by David J. Marcou.*
- *President Bush speaks, Onalasaka, October 2004, photo by Carole Edland.*

America's Dairyland

Patrick Slattery

Early years of the Engel family farm, Fountain City area, circa 1920, courtesy of the Werner and Jolene Engel Family.

America's Dairyland *is* Wisconsin—our license plates tell us as much. Wherever you go in the United States, mention Wisconsin and the usual response is talk about cows and cheese (or the Green Bay Packers). Interstate travelers along I-90/94, or even those who have never set foot in this land of milk and honey, are likely to think of Wisconsin as a handsome Eden.

When it comes to agricultural pursuits, Wisconsin is an especially fine place to sow and reap. Its green hue is due to the 30–plus inches of rainfall here annually. While only the southern third of the state is bona fide corn-belt country, what grows best in this state from north to south are forage crops—alfalfa, clovers, and grasses that are harvested as hay, whether by being ensiled, bagged,

Right: Laura Knoll feeding cows on her parents' farm, Sparta area, circa 1996, photo by Debbie Abraham.

Below: Hoeth family portrait, Hoeth farmstead, Goose Island, 1903, courtesy of the Don and LaVonne (Hoeth) Zietlow Family.

Charles Hass Dairy wagon in Oktoberfest parade, 2004, photo by Laurie Reed.

or baled. Cows' stomachs can transform these fibrous feeds into one of humankind's most valuable proteins—milk—and this bovine fermentation process makes possible one of Wisconsin's preeminent industries. The Northern Europeans, especially the Germans, who settled here in large numbers, had a long association with dairy cattle, and so it was a match made in heaven.

Dairy cows first came to the Americas with Christopher Columbus. Today, six main dairy cow breeds are raised in Wisconsin: Ayrshire, Brown Swiss, Guernsey, Holstein, Jersey, and Milking Shorthorn. From these cows flow 40 percent of the nation's cheese production and 20 percent of its butter. In the 1850s and '60s, John Smith and Chester Hazen developed the first widely marketable state cheeses, and 400,000 pounds of cheese were made in Wisconsin in 1859. Today, state cheesemakers turn out more than 2.1 billion pounds annually. More than three hundred varieties of cheese are made in Wisconsin, and it takes about ten pounds of milk to make one pound of cheese. England's and Wisconsin's favorite cheese, cheddar, was first made in the seventeenth century near Cheddar Gorge, Somersetshire, England.

Long before Wisconsin became known as a dairy state, wheat was the main cash crop. Early Yankee settlers brought their wheat-growing techniques with them to Wisconsin, supplying one-sixth of the wheat grown in the United States from 1840 to 1880. The chinch bug that hit the Baraboo area between 1858 and 1860 reduced farmers' wheat yields, and, along with depleted soil

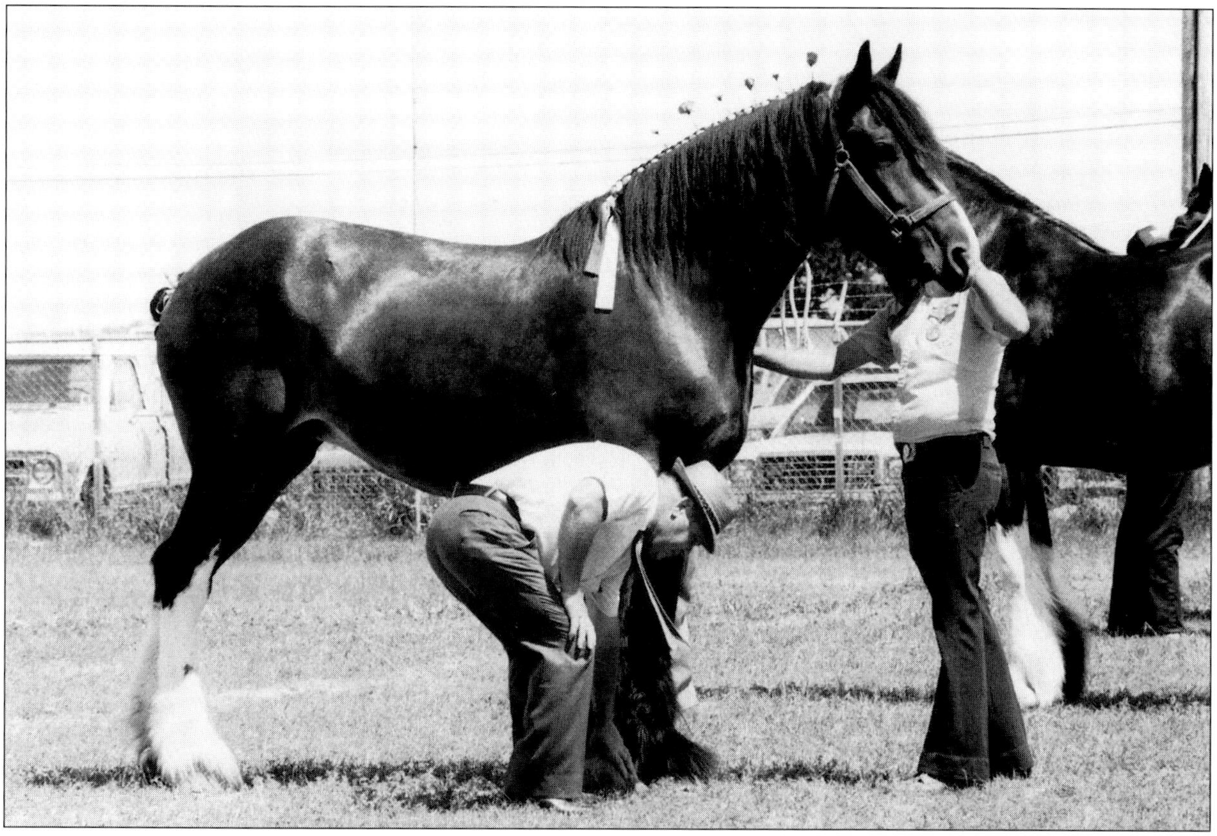

America's Dairyland 101

Top: Draft horse competition, Interstate Fair, 1980s, photo by Debbie Abraham.

Right: Filling up tractor, Vernon County Kwik Trip store, 2004, photo by Jim Solberg.

Horse, Amish buggies, and farm, Vernon County, 2004, photo by Professor Roger Grant.

and low prices, caused a change of course in Wisconsin's farming concentration. Dairying became the predominant agricultural enterprise south of where the forest took over (roughly, south of Highway 8 in the northern third of the state). As late as 1950, Wisconsin counted nearly 150,000 commercial dairy farms. Chickens, hogs, a few sheep, and beef cattle are also raised in the state, not to mention specialty animals like llamas, emus, and buffalo.

William Dempster Hoard (1836–1918) was instrumental in facilitating the shift from wheat to dairy farming by advocating the use of silos, refrigerated shipping, and government inspection of dairy products. His magazine, *Hoard's Dairyman,* reached tens of thousands of farmers nationwide. He also served as Wisconsin's governor from 1889 to 1891.

Today, Wisconsin's milk output continues to rise due to much more milk being produced per cow, although there are fewer cows and only about 15,000 dairy farms in the state at present. Along many rural roads, the empty barns far outnumber those that are still in business, and of the latter, many have expanded and modernized. The newly built dairies, with their milking parlors and free-stall barns, are far more complex in their operation than those used in the old red barns of the not-too-distant past.

Top: UW-Madison barn, 1930s, courtesy of the Werner and Jolene Engel Family.

Bottom: "Afghan" oat shocks, Vernon County, 2004, photo by Professor Roger Grant.

Farm silhouette at sunset, western Wisconsin, 1980s, photo by Terry Rochester.

Will only a few thousand dairy farms survive in Wisconsin? Some knowledgeable dairy experts say that's inevitable. But think of Wisconsin's wheat fields more than a century ago, and don't bet the farm that things can't change. Consider, for example, the tremendous rise of late in organic agriculture, a field in which Wisconsin plays a leading role, especially with Governor Jim Doyle's "Grow Wisconsin" initiative. The nation's largest organic cooperative, Organic Valley, is based in tiny La Farge in Vernon County.

Might the demand for beholding beautiful natural places make Wisconsin a worldwide green destination for tourists? Whatever the future holds, we can be certain that Wisconsin will forever be proud of its cows and the natural beauty of the land, and we are determined that it will always remain that way.

Annie Jerome, riding competitor, Interstate Fair, July 2002, photo by Peg Jerome, her mother.

106 Spirit of Wisconsin

THRESHING PARTY

For many generations, farmers have gathered to "thresh," a process whereby grain is separated from straw. The grain is used for food and the straw is now used for animal feed, although it was once also used to make mattresses, dolls, hats, etc. Father Michael Gorman, rector of La Crosse's St. Joseph the Workman Cathedral, grew up on his parents' farm in Richland County. His parents have passed away, but his family and friends still help him farm.

On September 4, 2004, their day began with a meal, followed by afternoon threshing, after everyone had gathered. Charlotte Nesseth, the Cathedral's liturgical coordinator, joined the group and enjoyed the day,

Threshing photos by Dennis McDonnell; badger photo by Jim Solberg.

You've seen this critter someplace before.

Health, Education, and Philanthropy

Kelly Weber

Physician's tools, Stonefield Village, circa 2000, photo by Paul Abraham.

Wisconsin's first hospitals were established in the early 1800s. Located at Fort Crawford in Prairie du Chien and Fort Howard in Green Bay—both built shortly after the War of 1812—the medicine practiced at them was rudimentary. Even Dr. William Beaumont, world-famous for his human digestion research, spent most of his time treating malaria caused by Fort Crawford's close proximity to the river, and could only conduct experiments during the winter.

Dr. Edwin Overholt, Gundersen-Lutheran, circa 2000, original painting by Peggy Baumgaertner.

Historic schoolroom, Stonefield Village, circa 2000, photo by Debbie Abraham.

But hospitals flourished in Wisconsin in the late nineteenth century. The state's first non-military hospital, St. John's Infirmary (now Columbia–St. Mary's), opened in Milwaukee in 1848. By 1900, there were fifty general hospitals in the state. The number of patients multiplied. When Madison General Hospital (now Meriter Hospital) opened in 1898, it had nine beds. In 1903, it saw 228 patients. In 1910, it saw 738. The hospital was overflowing and would need to add space eleven times over the next sixty years.

In that period, Wisconsin witnessed revolutionary medical advances. Medical professionals were developing areas of specialization to deal with the emerging complexities of practice. In more densely populated areas, doctors of different specialties often joined together in clinic-based groups to provide a variety of medical services to patients. In the 1920s, Wisconsin had more clinics than any other state in the country. Today, Wisconsin has 120 hospitals employing more than 212,000 healthcare professionals. Together, they see more than 12 million patients yearly.

Unlike medicine, education was slow to develop here. Although the first educational efforts by European settlers can be traced back to missionaries who accompanied fur traders in the mid-1600s, their primitive and often nomadic lifestyle created little need for formal education. In 1816, the two military forts were still the only places in the territory with organized schools. And it was

Health, Education, and Philanthropy 111

Mayor John Medinger with Cathedral School kindergarten students, circa 2001, courtesy of the John and Dee Medinger Family.

The Ranch, a vocational training organization for disabled youth, December 19, 1968, photo by Robert L. Miller for the Wisconsin Historical Society (ID#11446).

Visiting African professor Yaw Bredwa-Mensah, 2002, photo by Ronald S. Rochon, Ph.D.

not until 1849, against strong opposition, that Wisconsin's first free public school system began in Kenosha.

Institutions of higher learning also started slowly here, despite the basis for a system of higher education having been established in 1787. "Schools and the means of education shall forever be encouraged," wrote the creators of the Northwest Ordinance of 1787, which established the territory's governance. Familiar with East Coast universities like Harvard, which was 150 years old then, these early legislators knew the value of higher learning. However, it was another 63 years before the University of Wisconsin began. UW's first chancellor, John H. Lathrop, earned an annual salary of $2,000.

But Wisconsin had key national firsts. Margarethe Schurz, wife of German-American legislator and journalist Karl Schurz, opened the country's first kindergarten, in Watertown in 1856. The first vocational, technical, and adult education (VTAE) network began in Wisconsin in 1911, and its apprenticeship programs served as a model for federal legislation.

Today, Wisconsin has nearly 3,200 public and private elementary and secondary schools that stand as an example of educational excellence. The performance of the state's more than one million

Health, Education, and Philanthropy 113

Top: Father Roger Scheckel visiting a school for blind children partially sponsored by the La Crosse Diocese, Calcutta, India, 2004, courtesy of Father Scheckel.

Right: Gathering of western Wisconsin religious, educational, and philanthropic leaders, circa 2003, courtesy of the Drs. Robert and Carole Edland Family.

Frank Lloyd Wright's home and architectural school, Taliesin East, Spring Green, photo by Carl Liebig.

students has consistently ranked it among the smartest states in America. And 160,000-plus students are enrolled at the University of Wisconsin's 26 campus locations, along with numerous others at the state's many private universities and technical colleges.

The ultimate success of Wisconsin's health and educational systems is due, in large part, to the compassionate nature of its people. When Paul Samuel Reinsch, UW alumnus and former U.S. minister to China, was asked to describe the Wisconsin spirit in the 1920s, he spoke of its generosity and nurturing. "The broadening view of human relationships, the idea of the State as a big family, the devotion of the best talent therein to work for the general good, the testing of all rights by their just subservience to human welfare, these aims [are] so clearly expressed in the Wisconsin Idea," he said.

In fact, the philanthropy of Wisconsin is incredible. More than 30 percent of Wisconsin's families have reported charitable contributions on their tax returns over the past 10 years, and household giving increased by more than 60 percent from 1997 to 2002. Meanwhile, corporate donations accounted for more than 17 percent of the state's total charitable giving, well above the national average of 4.3 percent. Finally, this state contains more community foundations than any other American state. It is driven by the true spirit of Wisconsin.

Health, Education, and Philanthropy   115

Homeless Thomas Matty and a friend, western Wisconsin, 2004, photo by David J. Marcou.

Firsts and Bests

Nelda Liebig

We point with pride to pioneers who created firsts and bests in Wisconsin.

France's Louis XIV appointed Father Jacques Marquette to adventure with Louis Joliet; they discovered the Upper Mississippi River at present-day Prairie du Chien.

Jean Nicolet was probably the first European to view Lake Michigan. Thinking he'd reached China, at Green Bay, he stepped out of his canoe firing pistols, in Chinese damask robe.

Fort Clark, first fort on the Mississippi, was close to present-day Prairie du Chien and near today's historic Villa Louis, fur trader Hercules Dousman's mansion (now museum).

A group of fledgling legislators founded territorial Wisconsin's government in 1836, in Belmont, passing forty-two laws and establishing a judiciary. They established Madison as permanent capital, too.

In 1840, the settlement of Stanley's Tavern got a post office and permanent name. French trader Robert Grignon, desiring to befriend the Menominee, had the hamlet named for their chief, Oshkosh.

Statue of Jean Nicolet, the first European to view Lake Michigan and Green Bay, Red Banks, photo by Carl Liebig.

Left: U.S. flag, photo by Brett Vermeul.

Below: Little schoolhouse where the Republican Party was born, Ripon, photo by Carl Liebig.

Little Red Schoolhouse, where children learned reading, writing, and arithmetic until the 1960s, Wausau, photo by Carl Liebig.

On March 25, 1854, about fifty men met in a Ripon schoolhouse. Said one, "We went into the little meeting Whigs, Free Soilers, and Democrats. We came out Republicans, and we were the first Republicans in the Union."

In 1856, German immigrants Margarethe Moyer (Mayer) Schurz and husband Karl Schurz started the nation's first kindergarten, at Watertown.

In 1868, Christopher Latham Sholes of Kenosha and Milwaukee patented a time-saving device that changed writing forever—the typewriter.

A dubious claim to fame, Peshtigo's fire was the world's largest such loss of humans (more than a thousand), animals, property, and forests. In nearby Harmony, tombstones say, "Perished Oct 8, 1871." This holocaust happened the same day as the more famous but far less destructive Great Chicago Fire.

At Stony Hill School in tiny Waubeka, teacher Bernard J. Cigrand and his students held the first recognized "Flag Birth Day" on June 14, 1885. President Wilson proclaimed it a national observance on June 14, 1916.

In Oconto, north of Green Bay, stands a pretty frame building—the first church structure ever built for Christian Science services. Dedicated in 1887, it preceded the Mother Church of Boston by seven years.

Tombstone with the simple, omnipresent Peshtigo Fire date, Harmony, photo by Carl Liebig.

SS Meteor, *the last remaining whaleback ship, built in 1896 by Captain Alexander McDougall, photo by Carl Liebig.*

The whaleback ship *SS Meteor,* formerly the *Frank D. Rockefeller,* designed and built in 1896 by Alexander McDougall, is the last remaining whaleback. It's permanently berthed near Superior.

In 1899 salesmen John H. Nicholson and Samuel E. Hill met in Beaver Dam to help Christian travelers, forming the Gideons. Their volunteers still distribute scripture worldwide.

The state's oldest standing house is the Tank Cottage in Green Bay. Built in 1776 by Joseph Roi, a fur trader and one of Green Bay's first settlers, it was obtained in 1850 by Niels Tank, a rich Norwegian missionary. In 1908 the Tank Cottage was moved from along the Fox River to Tank Park, Mrs. Tank's gift to the city in memory of her husband. It now stands in Heritage Hill State Park.

Pendarvis House is a restored building in Mineral Point, the site of Wisconsin's first lead and zinc mine. Miners swarmed the hills, living in "badger holes," thus Wisconsin's nickname, the Badger State. In 1971, Mineral Point became the state's first city to be listed on the National Register of Historic Places.

In Ephraim, a 40 by 24-foot chapel was slowly winched up the hill from the lakeshore by means of horse and turntable. It is incorporated in the present-day Moravian church overlooking the village and bay.

It's often assumed that Harry Houdini, the great escape artist, was Appleton-born, a myth he perpetuated. He was actually born in Hungary; the family emigrated to Appleton when he was a toddler. He died of peritonitis from a ruptured appendix—not movie myth's underwater escape.

Top: Tank cottage, the oldest standing house in Wisconsin, built in 1776, Green Bay, photo by Carl Liebig.

Left: First Christian Science church built anywhere (1887), Oconto, photo by Carl Liebig.

Pendarvis House, a restored building in Mineral Point, the first Wisconsin city listed on the National Register of Historic Places, site of the state's first lead and zinc mine, where hillside shelters were called "badger holes," hence Wisconsin's nickname, photo by Carl Liebig.

Baraboo was site of the first Ringling Bros. show, in 1884. Baraboo's Circus World Museum long staged the largest history-based event in North America, the Milwaukee Circus Parade, now held in Baraboo.

One- and two-room schools operated here until the 1960s. The Little Red School House in Wausau is one such historic structure where dedicated teachers instructed rural children.

The thirty-seven-room Pabst Mansion is a Milwaukee jewel. Former sea captain Frederick Pabst, a beer baron, real estate developer, philanthropist, and arts patron, displayed pride in his German heritage. The 1890s were known as "The Pabst Decade" in Milwaukee.

A stand of old-growth white pine in Nicolet National Forest was a gift from Lucey Rumsey Holt, lumber baron W. A. Holt's wife. In the 1920s, she insisted that seventeen acres remain natural so

This building housed the country's first kindergarten, begun by immigrants Margarethe Moyer Schurz and her husband, Karl, Watertown, photo by Carl Liebig.

Christopher Latham Sholes of Kenosha and Milwaukee patented his invention, the typewriter, in 1868, and his daughter, Lillian, was the first typist, drawing courtesy of the Wisconsin Historical Society (ID#3196).

Roche-A-Cri State Park's most conspicuous and beautiful rock formation provides a seat for the Liebigs' daughter, Harriet (R), and friend, Adams County, photo by Carl Liebig.

future generations could see woods as they were before lumbering. A heron rookery now rests atop the pines.

Perhaps the most beautiful state rock is Roche-A-Cri in Adams County. And a tourist magnet is the Dells of the Wisconsin River. Boat tours move through narrow canyons, providing views of magnificent formations created by water and erosion.

Washington Island draws the most seekers of brilliant sunsets—the island is off the tip of Door County, and the sun sets over Green Bay.

The Pabst Mansion, built by Captain Frederick Pabst, a real-world renaissance man, Milwaukee, photo by Carl Liebig.

Sunsets off Washington Island in Door County draw tourists to the shores of Lake Michigan, photo by Carl Liebig.

Fests, Fairs, and Fun

Terry Rochester

Governor Tony Earl and the Circus Train, July 1985, photo by Dal Bayles.

If you try really hard in Wisconsin, especially from spring through fall, you can find a fest or fair to enjoy not only every weekend, but every DAY! Besides music fests and art fairs, we have fests celebrating cranberries, corn, apples, cherries, sunfish and catfish, sawdust, and yes (of course in Wisconsin), cheese and beer. And Milwaukee celebrates, well—just that it is Summer!

There are jazz fests, such as the Capital City Jazz Fest, in Madison in late April; La Crosse's Great River Jazz Fest held in August; and the Kettle-Moraine Jazz Fest, in West Bend (near Milwaukee) in September.

Right: Onalaska Anglers, a social club, Sunfish Days, Onalaska, circa 2000, courtesy of the Terry and Cheryl Smith Family.

Ella Fitzgerald at the Milwaukee Jazz Fest, late 1970s, photo by Terry Rochester.

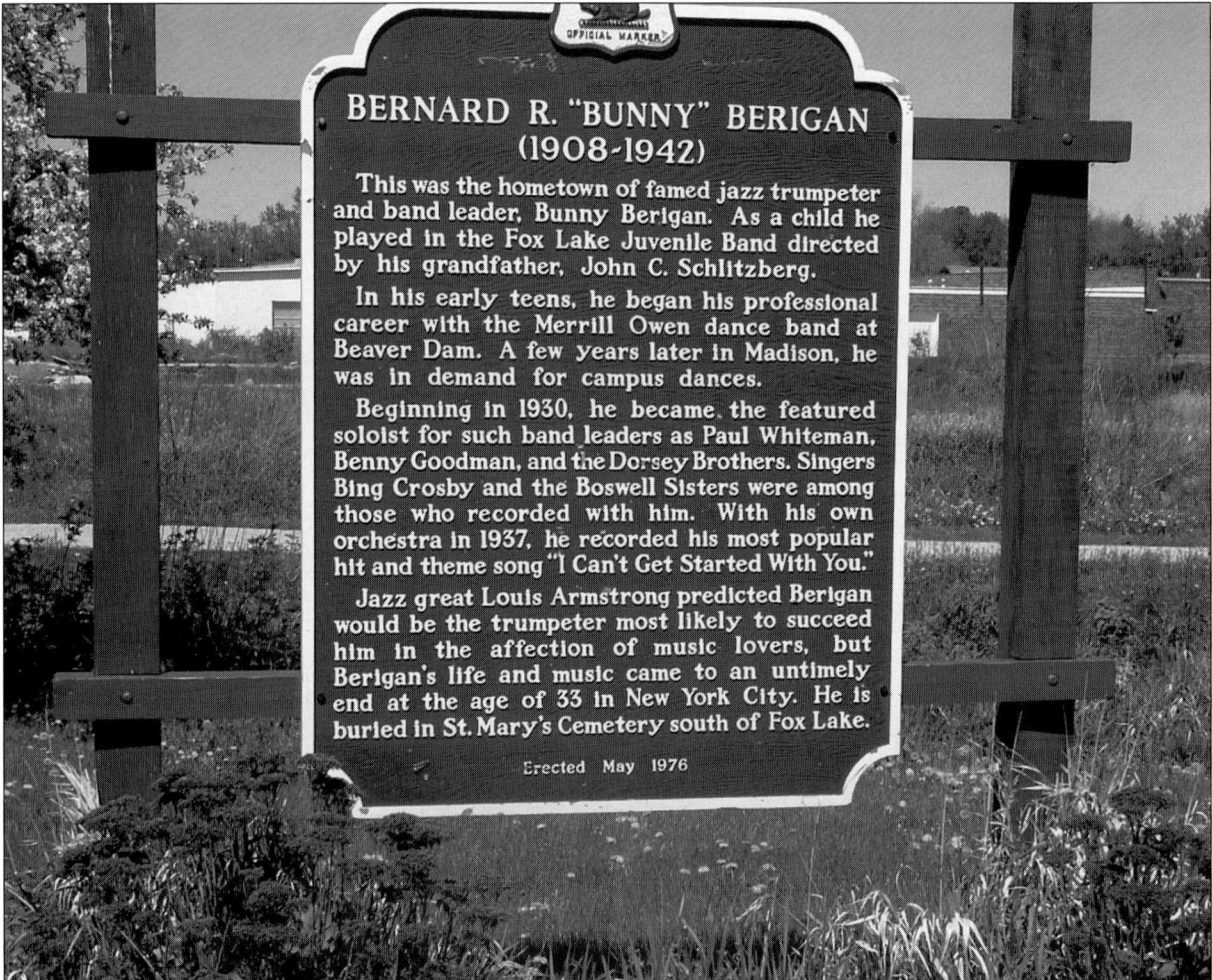

Bernard R. "Bunny" Berigan marker, a jazz legend remembered, near Fox Lake, photo by Sam McKay.

A bluegrass/gospel fest is held in Viroqua in July. Rock and country fests and several polka bashes are also held in the state throughout the summer.

There are folk fests, like the Great River Folk Fest in La Crosse—held the last weekend in August. Blues fests are held in Superior and Prairie du Chien (the Prairie Dog Blues Fest in July).

Summer outdoor art fairs are also prevalent in Wisconsin, including Milwaukee's Lakefront Festival of Arts in June; Madison's Art Fair off the Square in July; and La Crosse's Art Fair on the Green on the UW-La Crosse campus in July.

The largest music festival in the state is Summerfest in Milwaukee at the lakefront festgrounds, during a two-week period around July 4th.

Most of the other fests and fairs are seasonal. There are the Badger State Winter Games and the Snowflake Ski Club's International Ski Jump in February near Westby, where many Olympic skiers from around the world have jumped. And there is the Ghost Ships Festival in Milwaukee in February and the Flake Out Festival in Wisconsin Dells in January. Polar bear plunges also are held in various

Above: The Oktoberfest Singers, 2004, photo by tamara Horstman-Riphahn.

Below left: Giant Festival Foods shopping cart in Oktoberfest parade, 2004, photo by Laurie Reed.

Below right: Roberta and Mark Stevens, courtesy of the Stevens Family.

Kate Jerome with/in group photo display at the Wisconsin State Fair, circa 1997, photo by Peg Jerome.

parts of the state. The only other winter events are hard-core sports, the rec-fests, and camper, fishing, and building shows in bigger cities.

Outdoor fests and fairs begin in earnest in May, when one can be reasonably sure frost is not prevalent. One of the first events in spring is the Norwegian celebration of Syttende Mai, the seventeenth of May, with the usual great baked goods and handiwork. One of the largest celebrations is in Westby, where it seems that most people love to act Norwegian.

On the last weekend in May, Onalaska celebrates Sunfish Days. Many June Dairy Days celebrations occur in early June, with one of the largest in West Salem. Two large air fests draw big crowds: the International Experimental Fly-In Air Show in July in Oshkosh and the Deke Slayton Air Fest in La Crosse in June.

Then come many festivals that celebrate harvests of land and water—the State Fair in West Allis in August tops the list, plus River Fest in La Crosse around the 4th of July; Catfish Days in Trempealeau in July; the La Crosse Interstate Fair in July; the Northern Wisconsin State Fair in Chippewa Falls in July; and many county fairs throughout the state.

Other festivals include Kornfest in Holmen in mid-August; Apple Affair in Galesville in October; Sawdust Days in Altoona every summer; Strawberry Festival in Cedarburg in June; Cranberry Festival in Warrens in September; cherry blossom festivals in spring and harvest festivals in fall in Door County.

Fall brings the largest Oktoberfest outside Germany to La Crosse during a week and two weekends every early October.

CCC men play pool at Camp Nelson Dewey, now Wyalusing State Park, 1930s, courtesy of Paul and Lilly Kosir.

Gunfighter plane at the Oshkosh Experimental Fly-In, circa 1999, photo by Matthew A. Marcou.

Rising balloons, Coulee Region, photo by Debbie Abraham.

Many spectacular fireworks displays thrill observers on the Fourth of July, including those on Lake Shore during Summerfest in Milwaukee and in many other state towns and cities.

One of the longest traditions is the firing of pyrotechnics from Grandad Bluff in La Crosse at midnight every New Year's Eve. This endeavor has endured heavy winds, snow so heavy the fireworks could hardly be seen, and weather so frigid the fireworks hardly fired. But most years, it is a spectacular way to usher in the New Year for another annual round of fests, fairs, and fun in Wisconsin!

Fests, Fairs, and Fun 133

Fireworks, photo by Paul Abraham. Trio that can boost a fair, photo by Dave Larsen.

Seasons and Metaphors of Life

Essay by Karen K. List with Assistance on Captions from Anna Motivans.

A day in spring might be the first time you see a ladyslipper. Or at least it was for me. The winter's cold had gone so deep, I'd lost hope of seeing spring again, even by May. I was walking on a Door County trail with my yellow slicker pulled tight, trying to keep the raindrops from my eyes. And there it was beside me, fit only for a fairy's foot, a delicate yellow ladyslipper, bobbing at the end of a welcoming green stalk. I'd never seen one before. But there it was—proof that life was awakening, that even a thing as ethereal as this precious flower could bloom again. You wait for the day when the sun has warmed earth enough to lie flat on it—just as you would if you were making a snow angel in winter. And you lie stretched and still, letting the warmth from the ground radiate into your bones. A song drifts through your mind—"If I ruled the world, every day would be the first day of spring; every heart would have a new song to sing." You watch every living thing take its first deep breath, to be followed by blossoming, cavorting, singing those new songs and looking ahead to what life has in store. That could be anything, and everything.

Yellow ladyslipper, a nationally protected orchid species, Door County, photo by Sue Knopf.

Those fresh spring days are followed soon by summer's fullness. Or at least they were for me. I was sitting on a bluff overlooking the Mississippi near La Crosse; I could have sat there forever, watching the river roll by. The great thing about it is that the river moves, while you lie still and

Seasons and Metaphors of Life   135

Howard M. Temin Lakeshore Path, UW-Madison, 1930, photo by Melvin E. Diemer for the Wisconsin Historical Society (ID #24222).

Young dancers, universal spirit, photo by Jon Tarrant, British AWPA member.

The Wisconsin Singers, 2004, photo by Gary Coorough.

drink in the moment. You can afford the time now; summer is endless. "Summertime, and the livin' is easy." The breeze has warmth and heft enough to rock the blowsy pink peonies on their bushes and make the shade trees sway. Boats and clouds sail by. But you have the luxury to stay still, contemplate, put down roots, start your life's work with purpose and savor the time now and ahead when spring dreams come true. Even the Fourth of July and fireworks in Milwaukee don't rock your boat or shake your faith. Summer is endless, remember? Forever young.

Then comes fall and you wonder—how? Or at least I did. A drive down country roads shows green trees turning red, orange, yellow. Just a few leaves at first, and they, along with that first chill, always bring a pang of grief, since you know others will follow. Suddenly the radio is playing "September Song" and you hear it—"When the autumn weather turns the leaves to flame, one hasn't got time for the waiting game." You can scan to another station, but you can't stop the geese gathering on Horicon Marsh. You can't stop them from flying south again either. So when you hear their mournful honking and see the squirrels bustling through the yard, storing nuts against the cold, when you touch the frost on the pumpkins and see the corn in shocks, you know to hurry. You read in the newspaper

Seasons and Metaphors of Life 137

Left: Mike Carrell, traditional New Orleans jazz musician, photo by Sam McKay.

Below: UW-Madison tubas, most popular at home football games' "Fifth Quarter," photo by Gary Coorough.

Windmill, farm, sunset, Vernon County, 2004, photo by Professor Roger Grant.

that a woman just had twins at fifty-six, that a writer published her first novel at seventy, that eighty- and even ninety-year-olds are pumping iron and wearing high fashion. It must be true; you read it in the newspaper. So you force yourself to focus, step up the pace, store up accomplishments, large

Seasons and Metaphors of Life 139

Right: Stream and trees after heavy snowfall, Rhinelander area, photo by Gary Van Domelen.

Below: Rotary Christmas lights—a charitable fundraising activity, La Crosse, circa 2003, photo by Dave Larsen.

Hixon House, Christmas 2003, La Crosse, photo by Professor Roger Grant for the La Crosse County Historical Society.

and small, like a squirrel storing nuts against the winter, because all too soon winter is here. But something tells you, Life is still Good.

    I always knew when I took my winter walks by Madison's Lake Mendota that the ice went deep—to the other side of the world. I knew because I could feel it in those same bones warmed not long ago by the spring sun. Not much sunshine now. Only bitter cold and bodies wrapped up against it, so you forget what people look like. All living things now go to ground, taking their physical beings with them. Those who have wits about them hibernate. The rest pull their chairs closer to the woodstove and try to catch warmth. But there is dryness, brittleness, to this kind of heat. Still, you

Seasons and Metaphors of Life 141

Background: Easter children Sophia and Vince Bodoh, photo by Michelle Grenisen.

Top left: Father Roger Scheckel and his mother, Evelyn, courtesy of Father Scheckel.

Top right: Laurie's mother, Jeanne Reed, circa 2000, photo by Laurie Reed.

Sunflower, photo by Bob Mulock.

settle in and draw comfort, perhaps from where you're going, but more so from where you've been. "And in the gray of the morning," the Moody Blues sing, "my mind becomes confused between the dead and the sleeping and the road that we must choose." On those gray mornings, it's easy to forget whether someone is dead or sleeping or if it matters.

Then comes an instant when the ice is so thick, the cold so piercing, your reverie so deep, you're not even sure about you. Are you dead? Or sleeping? And while you're trying to decide, somewhere along a path in Door County, a yellow ladyslipper, fit only for a fairy's foot, appears at the end of a welcoming green stalk. And the world begins again, as it does for all who believe . . .

Seasons and Metaphors of Life   143

Oshkosh Experimental Fly-In smiley face, circa 1999, photo by Matthew A. Marcou.

UW-Madison Ph.D./UM-Amherst professor and writer Karen List, courtesy of Professor List.

Building Bridges of Destiny

Yvonne Klinkenberg

An old man and his grandson sat down one day after a walk, to talk,
And what they spoke was worthy of respect in how they taught and sought.

BOY: Grandfather, did you see the Capitol Building in Madison, standing straight and tall?
MAN: Grandson, did you stand on Grandad's Bluff, listening to an eagle call?
BOY: Look at the Blue Bridges stretching across the sky.
MAN: Or the geese that fly in a V-formation on high.
BOY: Look at all the stores, standing side-by-side.
MAN: And the prairie grass growing ever so wide.
BOY: Did you see the Milwaukee Zoo, filled with animals like the badger and bear?
MAN: Did you learn that you shouldn't surprise a beaver chomping on a poplar rare?
BOY: On interstate highways, we can ride wherever we want to go.
MAN: But on horseback, you can go fast or take it slow.
BOY: There's water in faucets to drink wherever we may be.
MAN: Yes, but the Mississippi once ran clear and cold for you and me.
BOY: Now you don't have to hunt and plant berries that are so sweet.
MAN: Yes, but we know what we need, and can follow the signs along trails to read.
BOY: Wouldn't you rather go to a store to buy?
MAN: No, we were born to Nature; we know how to live and die.
BOY: But look at the big hospital that could take care of us so.
MAN: But we know plants and herbs our women learned to grow.
BOY: We have a lot of fishing gear and boats to save us from care.
MAN: But you've never learned the patience to catch a fish with hands so bare.
BOY: But we have nets and coolers to keep the fish fresh.
MAN: But can you start a fire to cook them for a leafy dish?

Yes, the boy did listen as the old man talked.
Slowly, they stood up to take another walk.

MAN: Someday, Grandson, you will read all about the life I had; today I'm just an old man, half-sad. I was a Warrior Indian once, but today I am your Grandad.
BOY: But Grandad, without your wisdom, where would I be?
MAN: Grandson, go to what you call a Library. About us in Wisconsin my life and yours you will see. Use the pictures of the mind as if you were talking to me, of my life as a man and a place I once roamed free. Use your ears, eyes, and mind. Look at the pictures and you will always find, all your proud ancestors of yesterday and today. And know the growth of Wisconsin, the land, its people, and the fray, so when your grandchildren ask you what Wisconsin was like when... Help them, too, to understand. Red, yellow, black, and white—we all have to find the way that's right.
BOY: Thank you, Grandfather, I will. With our talks, I could never be still.
MAN: Grandson, remember the tone of my voice as much as the contents of my choice. Life needs bridges, and with you going ahead, the world will never wholly rid itself of... me and you... and our destiny of being read.